AUGUS

THE POETRY BOOKSHELF

General Editor: James Reeves

Robert Graves: *English and Scottish Ballads*
James Reeves: *Chaucer: Lyric and Allegory*
Tom Scott: *Late Medieval Scots Poetry*
William Tydeman: *English Poetry 1400–1580*
Martin Seymour-Smith: *Shakespeare's Sonnets*
Martin Seymour-Smith: *Longer Elizabethan Poems*
James Reeves: *John Donne*
Maurice Hussey: *Jonson and the Cavaliers*
Jack Dalglish: *Eight Metaphysical Poets*
James Reeves and Martin Seymour-Smith: *Andrew Marvell*
Dennis Burden: *Shorter Poems of John Milton*
V. de S. Pinto: *Poetry of the Restoration*
Roger Sharrock: *John Dryden*
James Reeves: *Jonathan Swift*
John Heath-Stubbs: *Alexander Pope*
Francis Venables: *The Early Augustans*
Donald Davie: *The Late Augustans*
Donald Davie: *Augustan Lyric*
F. W. Bateson: *William Blake*
G. S. Fraser: *Robert Burns*
Roger Sharrock: *William Wordsworth*
James Reeves: *S. T. Coleridge*
Robin Skelton: *Lord Byron*
John Holloway: *P. B. Shelley*
James Reeves: *John Clare*
Robert Gittings: *Poems and Letters of John Keats*
Edmund Blunden: *Alfred Lord Tennyson*
James Reeves: *Robert Browning*
James Reeves: *Five Late Romantic Poets*
Denys Thompson: *Poems and Prose of Matthew Arnold*
James Reeves: *Emily Dickinson*
James Reeves: *G. M. Hopkins*
David Wright: *Seven Victorian Poets*
James Reeves: *The Modern Poets' World*
James Reeves: *D. H. Lawrence*
James Reeves: *Thomas Gray*

AUGUSTAN LYRIC

*Edited with an Introduction
and Notes*

by

DONALD DAVIE

HEINEMANN
LONDON

Heinemann Educational Books Ltd
LONDON EDINBURGH MELBOURNE AUCKLAND TORONTO
SINGAPORE HONG KONG KUALA LUMPUR
IBADAN NAIROBI JOHANNESBURG
LUSAKA NEW DELHI

Distributed in the U.S.A. 1974 by
HARPER & ROW PUBLISHERS, INC.
BARNES & NOBLE IMPORT DIVISION

ISBN 0 435 15700 0 (cased)
ISBN 0 435 15701 9 (paper)

INTRODUCTION AND NOTES
© DONALD DAVIE 1974

FIRST PUBLISHED 1974

Published by
Heinemann Educational Books Ltd
48 Charles Street, London W1X 8AH
Printed in Great Britain by Morrison & Gibb Ltd
London and Edinburgh

CONTENTS[1]

	Page
INTRODUCTION	1

MATTHEW PRIOR (1664-1721)

On Exodus iii.14	31
To a Lady: She refusing ...	35
A Better Answer to Cloe Jealous	36
An Ode	38

ANNE FINCH, COUNTESS OF WINCHILSEA (1666-1720)

Life's Progress	39
A Nocturnal Reverie	41

ISAAC WATTS (1674-1748)

The Hardy Soldier	43
Few Happy Matches	44
Submission to Afflictive Providences	47
Life the Day of Grace and Hope	48
The Passion and Exaltation of Christ	49
Look on him whom they pierced, and mourn	50
Crucifixion to the World by the Cross of Christ	51
A Prospect of Heaven makes Death easy	52
The Church the Garden of Christ	53
Miracles at the Birth of Christ	54
Hosanna to Christ	55
The Shortness and Misery of Life	55

ANON

Admiral Benbow	57
*The Duke of Ormond's Health	58

[1] Note that several pieces are included for their curiosity or documentary interest, not for any intrinsic excellence. Such items are marked by an asterisk.

	Page
## JOSEPH ADDISON (1672-1717)	
Ode	61
## JOHN GAY (1685-1732)	
*Sweet William's Farewell to Black-Eyed Susan	63
Polyphemus's Song	65
Four Songs from *The Beggar's Opera*	66
## RICHARD GLOVER (1712-1785)	
*Admiral Hosier's Ghost	68
## HENRY CAREY (?1687-1743)	
*A Loyal Song	72
*He comes, he comes . . .	73
## CHARLES WESLEY (1707-1788)	
*He comes! he comes! the Judge severe . . .	74
Captain of Israel's Host and Guide	75
O Thou Eternal Victim slain	75
Wrestling Jacob	76
## JAMES THOMSON (1700-1748)	
Rule Britannia!	80
## WILLIAM COLLINS (1721-1748)	
Ode on the Death of Thomson	82
## PHILIP DODDRIDGE (1702-1751)	
Meditations on the Sepulchre in the Garden	84
*God's delivering Goodness acknowledged and trusted	85
## CHRISTOPHER SMART (1722-1771)	
A Morning Piece, Or an hymn for the hay-makers	87
A Noon-Piece, Or the Mowers at Dinner	89
Ode to Admiral Sir George Pocock	91
Hymn XIII. St. Philip and St. James	94

	Page
DAVID GARRICK (1717-1779)	
Hearts of Oak	98
JOHN WIGNELL	
*Neptune's Resignation	100
JOHN CUNNINGHAM (1729-1773)	
Morning	103
AUGUSTUS TOPLADY (1740-1778)	
A Living and Dying Prayer for the Holiest Believer in the World	105
JOHN NEWTON (1725-1807)	
Zion, or the City of God	106
WILLIAM COWPER (1731-1800)	
This ev'ning, Delia, you and I	108
Light Shining out of Darkness	109
Welcome Cross	110
Self-Acquaintance	111
The Shrubbery, Written in a Time of Affliction	112
On the Trial of Admiral Keppel	113
The Modern Patriot	113
Joy and Peace in Believing	114
Jehovah our Righteousness	116
Exhortation to Prayer	117
Prayer for Patience	118
Welcome to the Table	119
Love Constraining to Obedience	120
The Valley of the Shadow of Death	121
The Negro's Complaint	122
Sweet Meat has Sour Sauce	124
*A Good Song	125
To Mary	127

	Page
EOGHAN RUADH O SUILLEBHAIN (1748–1784)	
*Rodney's Glory	130
PRINCE HOARE (1775–1835)	
*The Arethusa	133
THE EARL OF MULGRAVE (1755–1814)	
'Our line was form'd'	135
WILLIAM BLAKE (1757–1827)	
Song	137
COMMENTARY AND NOTES	139
INDEX OF AUTHORS	177
INDEX OF TITLES AND FIRST LINES	178

For Donald Greene
fellow-enthusiast

INTRODUCTION

I

Chronology

This anthology is concerned, not quite but almost exclusively, with one kind of poetry written in England between the death of Dryden in 1700 and the appearance in 1790 of William Blake's *Songs of Innocence*. The second of these dates hardly needs to be justified; for whatever we take 'lyric' to mean, we know that it describes the *Songs of Innocence*, and yet whatever we take 'Augustan' to mean, we know that it does not describe William Blake. On the other hand 'Augustan' certainly fits, as has been widely acknowledged (not least in the eighteenth century), poems written by Dryden and others in the last thirty or forty years of the seventeenth century; and some of those poems, by explicitly offering themselves as 'Song' or 'Ode' or 'Hymn', demand to be categorized as 'lyric'. It has to be explained why these poems have been excluded.

To explain, we have to go outside strictly literary history. There is a current tendency to decry what the eighteenth century called 'the Glorious Revolution' of 1698, which effectively though not immediately ousted the Stuart dynasty; and to present instead, as the only *true* revolution that the English have experienced (or at least as the nearest that they ever came to that allegedly rejuvenating experience), the Civil War of 1642–49, together with the Cromwellian interregnum which succeeded it. If we measure in terms of blood spilled, or of emotional temperature, this may well be right. But if we measure in terms of *consequences*, we must think that the eighteenth century was right in regarding the Revolutionary Settlement of 1698 as much more momentous than the regicide of 1649. At the risk of simplifying grossly, it may be said that the

Revolutionary Settlement acknowledged that England had become or was fast becoming, a bourgeois and mercantile society. And the writers of the Restoration period were only fitfully aware of this; for the most part their writings assume a society which is aristocratic, and monarchical in the thoroughgoing sense that the monarchy is taken to be naturally and essentially absolute. Both assumptions were challenged, and in effect overthrown, by the Revolutionary Settlement.

Accordingly, whereas in Restoration comedy and lyric the merchant figures largely as potential cuckold, his wife and daughters appearing only to be seduced by the aristocratic rake, in post-revolutionary literature the merchant (Addison's Sir Andrew Freeport) is on the contrary a figure of great consequence, and his womenfolk must be treated with flattering attention and civility. And this is an accurate reflection of what seem to have been the facts of economic and political life: the land-owning aristocrat could survive and keep his privileges only if he allied himself with the mercantile interests—an alliance which is the basis of the Whig hegemony throughout most of the eighteenth century. The monarch, so far from being absolute, could survive only so long as he acknowledged that the effective power rested with this allegiance between the landed and the commercial interests. And the code of manners, by which the Duchess of Newcastle and the wife of the lately knighted London merchant could when necessary communicate on stately terms without embarrassment, was worked out and disseminated in *The Spectator* by those journalists of genius and social responsibility, Addison and Steele. It is not a mere change in the ruling dynasty, but on the contrary this momentous switch from a predominantly aristocratic to a predominantly middle-class society, which requires us for our purposes to take as starting-point 1700 or 1698 rather than 1660.

And at the other end of our span, it is not until 1790 that English imaginations, like William Blake's or Joseph Priestley's, began to conceive, faced with the spectacles of first the American and then the French revolutions, that the liberties ensured by the Glorious

Revolution were not altogether real, or not altogether comprehensive; to conceive the possibility of an industrial rather than a mercantile economy, and of a popular rather than a bourgeois democracy.

II

'*Lyric*'

We get a slanted image of the English eighteenth century when we approach it by way of the greatest literary imaginations of the period. For it so happens that what are arguably the most intense and passionate writers of the century—Pope and Swift in the first half, Johnson and Goldsmith in the second—were profoundly reactionary minds. All four were, in different degrees, out of sympathy with the Whiggish England that they were born to—commercial as that was, expansionist, dynamic, technologically inventive and confident. Tories in a world of Whigs, they were in the strictest sense 'radicals'—though of the Right; their criticisms of their society went to the roots, asking *why* social mobility, *why* territorial and commercial expansion, *why* conspicuous consumption, should be accepted as self-evident symptoms of national health and vigour. And so it is not surprising, though it is ironical, that the twentieth-century radical of the Left should find it relatively easy to sympathize with, and admire, an eighteenth-century radical of the Right such as Johnson; both are critics of capitalist imperialism, one before the fact, the other after it.

In the nature of the case, however, these could not be *lyrical* imaginations. For the profoundly radical and reactionary imagination, the natural mode and vehicle is the critical mode of attire. And precisely because, in the satirist, imagination is in this way not so much active as *re-active*, old-fashioned readers at least since Matthew Arnold have found it hard to allow to satire anything but an inferior status among the exertions and endeavours of poetry. Where the eighteenth century is concerned this prejudice, though it persists more widely than we care to acknowledge, has come under so much fire from leaders of opinion that it has largely gone underground. There are many more people who think that Pope is not truly a poet at all, than there are people prepared to stand up and say so.

What has been taken for granted, by both parties to this muffled argument, is that the case for our eighteenth-century poetry must rest upon a recognition not just, right enough, that the satire (along with related kinds like the epistle) is an honourable and noble form; but also that the reader whose ideal of true poetry is Shelley or Gerard Manley Hopkins or George Herbert must cast aside such prejudices and expectations when he engages with the poetry of the eighteenth century. In other words, whatever the virtues of the poetry of that century, it is assumed that they cannot be lyrical virtues.

And yet how can that be? If, as I have argued, the characteristic temper of the English eighteenth century is expansive and confident (everything that Pope and Swift, Johnson and Goldsmith, were not), how can it be that this temper is not expressed in its poetry? Were *all* the poets Tories, not a Whig among them? Once the question is put in that form, it will be seen that there was, there *must have been*, lyrical poetry in the eighteenth as in any other century. And in fact, if we take 'lyrical' in this extended sense to comprehend whatever is sanguine, positive and excited, the century has a great lyrical poet in James Thomson (1700–48), author of *The Seasons*, of *Liberty*, and of 'Poem to the Memory of Sir Isaac Newton'. For Thomson's was an imagination which responded with elation and wonderful vividness to the enlarged horizons opened up by maritime expansion and traffic on the one hand, on the other hand the discoveries and applications of Newtonian science.

However, I have tried to take 'lyric' in a narrower sense, to mean *a poem composed either to match an existing piece of music, or in the expectation and hope of a musical setting being contrived for it*. And this rules out all of Thomson's important poems except 'Rule, Britannia' (which last, however, reads very differently in the context I have just sketched for it than when it is taken to be a piece of patriotic sabre-rattling, heartlessly produced to order).

I have excluded also the poet whom a reader in 1788 declared to be 'the greatest lyrist the world has produced'. This was Thomas Gray. His incautious admirer was the poetess Anna Seward, and the performances by Gray which she had in mind were undoubtedly his Pindaric Odes. The Pindaric Ode, a form much practised throughout the century and particularly in its later decades, is without doubt one kind of lyric, and for mostly excluding such poems I can plead only practical considerations: the more famous examples, by Gray and others, are readily available elsewhere; they require a frame of mind not appropriate to poems I'm more concerned the reader should respond to; and finally, they would have taken up too much room.

For, so far from eighteenth-century lyrics being hard to find, there is an embarrassment of riches. 'Rule, Britannia', 'Hearts of Oak', 'Rock of Ages', 'Guide me, O Thou great Jehovah', ''Twas when the seas were roaring', 'When I survey the wond'rous cross', 'Gentle Jesus, meek and mild', 'Here's to the maiden of bashful fifteen', 'All in the Downs the fleet was moor'd', 'God moves in a mysterious way', 'Here, a sheer hulk, lies poor Tom Bowling', 'How doth the little busy bee', 'Let dogs delight to bark and bite', 'Jesu, lover of my soul'—each of these (and the list could be three times as long) turns out to be an eighteenth-century lyric, as I have defined it. And that Englishman or Englishwoman has had a deprived childhood, who does not remember one or two out of this list as somehow familiar. Not all of them by any means, once the words are abstracted from the catchy tune that comes to mind along with each of them, stands up as a poem in (as we oddly say) 'its own right'. And accordingly not all of them appear in these pages. Yet 'its own right' is a strange conception when applied to poems that are, in the strictest sense, lyrics; for, almost by definition, such a poem asks to be judged as only one half of a total experience of which the other half is the tune that we sing it to. Moreover, in cases where we know the tune (or *some* tune), abstracting the words from the tune, if it is legitimate, is not always in practical experience possible. And it varies greatly from one reader to the

5

next—not just because of native aptitudes, but because of different experience.

Take the case of the congregational hymn. The eighteenth century is the great age of English hymn-writing, the century of Watts and Wesley, Newton and Cowper. A reader who is used, in church or chapel, to sing 'Christians, awake!' or 'Glorious things of thee are spoken', will find it much harder to consider the hymns as poems, as exclusively verbal constructions, than will the reader who never worships. (On the other hand, presumably, the Christian reader will be more in sympathy with what the hymns, as poems, *say*.) I have tried to get round this difficulty, and to let all readers start equal, by printing mostly hymns that are seldom sung.

III

'*Augustan*'

But with an anthology where, as now appears, the hymns of the Christian churches must figure largely, what happens to the promise implicit in the word, 'Augustan'? Surely the point the hymns enforce is that, in this century which we call unthinkingly 'neo-classical', the imagination of the English of all ranks is peopled by figures and events from the Hebrew scriptures at least as much as by personalities and stories from Graeco-Roman mythology, history and literature. True enough; and it is hard to think of a point that is more worth making. Yet the truth is that the most influential and famous hymn-writers—Watts, the Wesleys, Cowper—were very good and cultivated Latinists; and that the precedent of Horace above all was as compelling for them as for the secular poets their contemporaries.

It is Horace above all who matters; the Horace of the *carmina*. For the pre-Augustan Catullus, the eighteenth century as a whole had less liking than the seventeenth century before it or the nineteenth century after. And though Thomson and others at mid-century imitated Tibullus, as others imitated Anacreon and Pindar, it is the Horace of the *carmina* (the 'odes') who stands for most of the eighteenth century as the type of the lyric poet.

It is just here that it becomes important to take the measure of Matthew Prior who, not at all by accident, stands first in this anthology. For the eighteenth century, and we must suppose for Prior himself, his most important poem was his most ambitious, *Solomon on the Vanity of the World*, of which Charles Wesley in 1778 required his daughter Sally to get the first book by heart. Henry Bett has shown that *Solomon* was so constantly in the minds of the Wesleys that it is literally impossible to account for every turn of phrase which Prior's poem contributes to the Wesleys' hymns. However *Solomon* is in no sense a lyrical poem, and so Prior as a religious or devotional poet is represented here by his Ode, *On Exodus iii.14*, which the Wesleys esteemed not much less than *Solomon*. (See the notes to this poem for a demonstration that the disrepute into which Prior has fallen as a religious poet—he does not figure in Dame Helen Gardner's *Book of Religious Verse*—is undeserved.) Nevertheless, the Horatian Prior whom the eighteenth-century poets esteemed, sacred and secular poets alike, is not the religious poet but the author of, for instance, 'A Better Answer to Cloe Jealous'. This poem is printed in one anthology after another, yet no one undertakes to explain what claim it has on our attention, so manifestly trivial as it is in subject-matter. It is prudent and proper not to break butterflies on wheels; yet it will not do to label this poem 'charming', and leave it at that. Nearly forty years ago F. R. Leavis in his *Revaluation* showed how to account for the distinction of not dissimilar pieces of bantering gallantry by Thomas Carew and Andrew Marvell. Their value and their achievement, Leavis said, was in their tone; though what the voice said was trivial, by its tone the voice in the poem displayed *urbanity*. And urbanity, the Horatian virtue, was a very serious matter for these poets and their first readers, as it should be for us; for it is neither more nor less than tact and sympathy and sureness in the handling of human relations within the decorous proprieties insisted on by a civilized society. Leavis showed how the touch was lost, how good breeding coarsened into mere raffishness, in poems of gallantry written after the Restoration. What can be claimed for Prior is that at his hands the valuable urbanity was regained—yet with a difference, all the difference involved in passing from an aristocratic to a bourgeois society. This is to claim for Prior in verse what has been often claimed for Addison and Steele in prose. Women's Liberation may prefer the 'Madam' or 'Lady' of aristocratic address to Prior's 'child' and 'girl'; undoubtedly in the transition certain finenesses were lost, and it may indeed be true that privileged women in the upper orders of Elizabethan and Caroline society enjoyed more equality *vis-à-vis* their menfolk than did the wives and daughters and mistresses of the eighteenth-century middle class (though those women sought and achieved more equality as the century wore on). Yet a poem like 'A Better Answer' or 'To a Lady: She Refusing . . .' certainly affords a valuable model of how to handle relations between the sexes with civility and finesse. If we look at Prior's Horatian poems as so many model performances in the conduct of human relations, in using social conventions so as to steer and enrich such relations rather than stifle them, we cannot fail to be impressed by Prior's range; not just how a man should behave towards his wife or his mistress, but how a grown man should treat a girl-child, how a bachelor should treat his housekeeper (as in the admirable and surprising 'Jinny the Just', too little known since its first publication in 1907), how a man should treat his colleague, his drinking-companion, his patron—these are the problems, if that is the word, to which Prior addresses himself. The more trivial the overt subjects or occasions, the more the lesson goes home, for what is involved is precisely *nuance*, a nicety of human attention for which no occasion (a tiff, a fit of the sulks, an awkwardly discontinued conversation) is too trivial to be worth taking care about. And thus, at the end of the 'Better Answer', the explicit appeal to Horace is intended seriously, for all that it is touched upon so lightly; there are sides to Horace in the *carmina* which are outside Prior's range altogether, but Horace's urbanity is what Prior can respond to very acutely, and can emulate with great resourcefulness.

Intimately related, and even more to the point if we are concerned with Prior's legacy to his successors, is the line:

> Let us e'en talk a little like folks of this world.

Much more than is commonly acknowledged, eighteenth-century poetry *does* talk 'like folks of this world'; and indeed a main intention of this anthology is to show how much of it does so. Of poets not represented here, Swift almost throughout, and Pope much of the time, use a language that is conversational, not to say colloquial; and one can only suppose that those people have not read Pope who declare confidently to the contrary. As the century wore on, however, the language of poetry became more divorced from the language that was spoken; though there are striking exceptions like Cowper, and one has to distinguish between Johnson and Goldsmith, who admitted spoken usage as a relevant consideration, and poets like Gray, who did not. To hymn-writers like Watts and the Wesleys and Cowper, themselves learned and sophisticated men who sought for their hymns a diction meaningful to unlearned congregations, Prior's precedent in talking 'a little like folks of this world' was momentous. And this explains why Cowper should have exploded in indignation at Johnson's treatment of Prior in his *Lives of the Poets*, and why John Wesley should have printed in his *Arminian Magazine*, though to the scandal of some of his followers, Prior's ballad, 'Henry and Emma', which Johnson the High Churchman thought improper. It explains why Isaac Watts, not much less than the Wesleys and Cowper, drew on Prior's precedent; and why John Wesley towards the end of his life should have sprung to Prior's defence with his *Thoughts on the Character and Writings of Mr. Prior*. The devotional poets recognized their debt to Prior, and repaid it in admiration. And since Prior in his secular poems quite often skirts impropriety, we begin to see that the eighteenth-century hymn-writers were not such blinkered and inflexible dogmatists as we tend to suppose.

IV

Ballads

A very different matter is the other body of popular poetry which I have tried to represent. In church or chapel the unlettered eighteenth-century Englishman could be nourished, at least some of the time, by a poetry like the poetry of Horace; by language that was clean, solid and intellectually sinewy, as well as forcefully melodious. In the theatre or the taproom, though Boreas and Amphitrite and Gallia and Albion swirled neo-classical draperies about the patriotic words that he sang or had sung to him, these were excrescences upon a form, the ballad, which owed nothing to precedents in Latin or Greek. In the eighteenth century the ballad was understood to be at least as much lyric as narrative, as we see when John Gay calls his masterpiece 'a ballad-opera'. However *The Beggar's Opera* is in English a unique achievement; and it would be generally agreed that the street-ballad of the eighteenth century is a sadly degenerate relative of those ballads of the Anglo-Scottish border which we think of as the classics of this form. One can always be asked to imagine that in the eighteenth as in any other century, in field or market or at the quay-side, the 'people' was composing, and singing or reciting, poems more truthful and affecting than the poems of the literate *élite* which we read from the printed page. But the trouble is that on this argument any example of this poetry which is put before us has to be inferior, because it has to be had corrupted into print before we can look at it. Accordingly we have a duty to be sceptical; the naval ballads which I have chosen to represent the popular ballad in general turn out to be not *by* 'the people' but *for* them; or else, if some of them had a source that was genuinely of the people, like the 'fore-bitters' that we know were composed and sung on the men-o'-war, that original has been transformed and dressed up to please a wider audience, before ever the piece comes down to us. This is not to say that they are all of a piece; on the contrary, David Garrick's 'Hearts of Oak' (p. 98) is seen for the humane and true if modest achievement that it is, when set beside John Wignell's 'Neptune's Resignation' (p. 100), which I have rescued from oblivion chiefly so as to show how bad an eighteenth-century lyric could be.

What this material can cure us of is the not uncommon self-pitying supposition that ours, 'the TV age', is the first in which the media of communication have been manipulated so as to feed us, 'the people', with entertainment that is manifestly insulting to us, trashy and dishonest. The printed page is a medium no less than the television network, and indeed when print takes the form of 'broadsides', as it commonly did for the topical ballads (see Pinto and Rodway, *The Common Muse*), we may say that it is a *mass*-medium. Charles Dibdin (1745–1814) had a career as a purveyor of mass-entertainment such as we too readily suppose has been possible only in our own times or in the past hundred years. In the eighteenth century as in ours what is offered as 'art of the people' turns out to be that very different thing, art directed at the populace by promotors who seek a wide sale, or else art wished on the populace by those who have a recruiting-sergeant's interest in offering themselves as 'the people's' spokesmen.

A much more respectable name than Dibdin's is smirched by this sort of imputation; for 'Sweet William's Farewell' by Gay (p. 63) is rather plainly, when we look at it, heartlessly patronizing. Gay's talent was for the burlesque; and just as his *Shepherd's Calendar* fitfully achieves the pastoral note by setting out to be mock-pastoral, so *The Beggar's Opera* achieves the heroic while intending only the mock-heroic. Thus it may be that 'Sweet William's Farewell' was intended to burlesque certain genuine ballads, on much the same lines as Gay's broader and less interesting burlesque, ''Twas when the seas were roaring'. But in either case we surely have to say that the burlesque was misconceived and cheap, in a way that no incidental felicities ('So the sweet lark, high-pois'd in air/Shuts close his pinions to his breast') can compensate for. And more generally, when Horatian urbanity is thus reduced to an ironical formula for eating one's cake and having it (the manoeuvre is practised by twentieth-century poets as well), we have a duty to refuse the bargain. I am confessing to a distrust of Gay's motives which will explain why, accomplished and sensitive as he is, he figures in this collection less largely than might have been expected.

Gay's failure is excusable and symptomatic. Though in earlier periods there had been literature directed at the mercantile or artisan middle-class—for instance, in the Jacobean period, Thomas Deloney's romances and Dekker's plays—the social revolution registered by the Revolutionary Settlement demanded a re-thinking of artistic categories so wholesale that such precedents were hardly helpful. Literary theory since the Renaissance had assumed that the middle and lower classes in society could figure in the national literature, except in specially class-oriented *genres* like Deloney's narratives, only under the aegis of *comedy*. 'Sweet William's Farewell' shows Gay trapped in this assumption, struggling to overcome or circumvent it, but ultimately defeated. It's in the light of this defeat that the mid-Victorian anthologist, F. T. Palgrave, was splendidly right to single out for posterity 'Sally in Our Alley' by the obscure and unhappy Henry Carey, as succeeding where the infinitely more gifted poet, Gay, had failed—in giving a touching and unaffected image, without condescension, of how human sentiments and relations worked out among the lower orders. Carey's poem has been anthologized many times since, seldom with any sense so sure as Palgrave's of what its claim on our attention consists in. Because it is thus readily available, I have omitted it.

The Beggar's Opera represents not a solution of this problem, but an evasion of it; for by setting his action in the criminal classes (among whom the class-structure of law-abiding society is kaleidoscopically mingled, rather than inverted), Gay brilliantly circumvented the problem of how to make artisans and merchants as much the objects of human concern as were fine lords and ladies. And accordingly, as William Empson and others have shown, *The Beggar's Opera*—suavely central though it is to English Augustan literature—in fact finds its progeny in Romantic literature, in a literature which assumes that honesty and humanity are to be found not anywhere in the interstices of the social order but only outside that order, among the outlaws, the 'cop-outs'.

V

Four Poets

Rather than represent non-lyrical poets by uncharacteristic lyrical effusions (Pope by the 'Ode: on Solitude' and the 'Universal Prayer'; Swift by 'The Day of Judgment'; Johnson by 'A Short Song of Congratulation'; Goldsmith by a song from *The Vicar of Wakefield*), I have chosen to devote space rather to certain eighteenth-century poets whose genius was indeed lyrical, to a degree that I think is still unacknowledged. I name four such poets: Watts, Smart, Cowper, John Newton. (A fifth, Charles Wesley, certainly deserves no less of me and of my readers; but Wesley's claims must await another time and another hand.)

ISAAC WATTS

The English puritan, that figure which, however we apprehend it, must figure so largely in any account that we give of our seventeenth century—what happens to him when the seventeenth century becomes the eighteenth? If we asked ourselves that question (it seems we seldom do), we should collide at once with the massive figure, and the formidably single-minded career, of Dr. Isaac Watts.

We may say that the puritan became respectable—less by acceding to the standards of society, than by making those standards bend to his. But this is inadequate. With Watts the English puritan became not just respectable, but (the more pregnant and momentous term that the eighteenth century set store by) he became *civil*. He contrived, in Watts's time and with Watts's help, to enter into, and take his share of, Augustan secular culture—and all without bending the rigour of his principles.

It's important to realize that many puritans remained within the Church of England. John Norris for instance, who helped to form Watts's literary opinions (see Norris's *Collection of Miscellanies*, 1706), was rector of Bemerton. And later in the century, if the Evangelical movement was a puritan movement (as it surely was), most of its leading figures—John Newton, Toplady, the Wesleys themselves—remained inside the Established Church. The puritan is not to be identified with the dissenter or, as we mostly call him today, the nonconformist. But because dissenters were, like the Papists, debarred by law from many areas of the national life (for instance from the universities—the dissenters in consequence created their own alternative educational establishment, in many ways more liberal than Oxford and Cambridge), it is among the dissenters like Watts that we get the strongest sense of a culture within a culture, distinct from the national culture yet not insulated from it.

The process was traced by Max Weber and later R. H. Tawney by which the Puritan principles (frugality, regularity, sobriety, diligence), since they were also the requirements for commercial success, in due course and in many cases brought worldly rewards to those whose hopes were set (so they would have said, and no doubt sincerely) upon another world altogether. By Watts's time the fruits of this happy coincidence were there for the gathering in; and by 1700 a great deal of the commerce and finance of the City of London, as of provincial centres like Bristol, Hull and King's Lynn, was in the hands of the dissenters. But this is due not solely to the puritanism which the dissenters shared with many anglicans, but to the statecraft which had deliberately diverted into commerce the dissenting talent and energy which might have gone into government. At any rate, these dissenters were among those merchants with whom the Whig landowners had to combine if they were to keep their privilege and status. The dissenters were the implacable though sober zealots for whom maintaining the Whig hegemony was a matter of life and death; who would have plunged England into renewed civil war rather than see a Tory administration, just as some of Swift's associates in the brief Tory administration of 1712–13 were prepared to deal with the Pretender, as their only hope of regaining the power that they lost with Queen Anne's death. Each knew his enemy: Swift, whose whole career makes sense only if we see it directed at such as Watts; and Watts, whose loyal poem of 1705 to Queen Anne was given a vicious 'Palinodia' in 1721, because the Queen had let in the Tories ten years before.

It would be charitable to say that Watts as poet has been the victim of his own success; that we take so much for granted the rhetoric of the English congregational hymn that we never pause to wonder who created that rhetoric. (Watts did, almost single-handed.) But we ought not to be so charitable, not to ourselves nor to our mentors of this and of preceding generations. For the curiously ambiguous status of Isaac Watts as poet—his figuring modestly in all respectable anthologies and a great deal more largely in our oral tradition, yet never remembered as one in the succession of our illustrious poets—reflects, one cannot help but think, a similar ambiguity in the official or received version of English culture when it comes to assessing the contribution to that culture of puritanism in general and of nonconformists in particular. The roundheads of Cromwell are remembered as the iconoclasts who defaced the sculpture of our churches; Watts and his associates are thought of as comically illiberal because they supported (as Prior did also) Jeremy Collier's successful protest against the licentiousness of the Restoration theatre; dissenters of a later day are remembered as Matthew Arnold's 'philistines'; and in our own day the non-conformists are said to have influenced, for good or ill, far more than Karl Marx the cast of mind of the British Labour Party. Particularly puerile are attempts to explain English nonconformity, along with brass bands and whippet-racing, as a product of something called (if you please) 'working-class culture'. One looks in vain for any general recognition that the artistic culture of the nation, so far from being repudiated by nonconformists as the product of a ruling class or an alien caste, has been embraced by the best of them in every generation, and enriched (though also at times valuably purged) by their efforts. Isaac Watts is the unavoidable representative of that embrace and that enrichment.

When A. E. Housman, in *The Name and Nature of Poetry* (1933), quotes four lines of Watts and comments, 'That simple verse, bad rhyme and all, is poetry beyond Pope', this is worse than useless. It suggests, and is meant to suggest, that there is an artless tradition represented by Watts, which is a superior alternative to an artful tradition represented by Pope. No such thing! Watts is a very artful poet, and his simplicity is the product of art. (It is also the product of a heroic abnegation by this poet of the splendours and artifices which he could deploy, and had, in his earliest pieces—see his 'Few Happy Matches', p. 44.) Isaac Watts is a great poet by precisely those standards that make Pope a great poet. This is not to say he is as great as Pope; that would be absurd. But it does mean that, hymn-writer as he mostly though not exclusively is, Watts represents not an alternative tradition but the one unavoidable tradition of English poetry. In his hymns and out of them he writes solidly, cleanly and sparely. This is what we say of Pope; and it is what we have to say, if we are honest, of Watts.

This point must be emphasized, and not just in relation to Watts. In Henry Bett's admirably learned and indispensable book, *The Hymns of Methodism*, perhaps the single wrong note is struck when, discussing the importance of Prior for the Wesleys, Bett says (p. 159), 'It was his influence that saved them from the monotonous antithesis of the "correct" style of Pope.' There is a letter from John Wesley (to the Reverend Mr. Furley, July 15, 1764) which shows that Wesley could hardly have agreed with this:

> If you imitate any writers, let it be South, Atterbury, or Swift, in whom all the properties of a good writer meet. I was myself once much fonder of Prior than Pope; as I did not then know that stiffness was a fault. But what in all Prior can equal, for beauty of style, some of the first lines, that Pope ever published?—
>
>> Poets themselves must die, like those they sung,
>> Deaf the praised ear, and mute the tuneful tongue;
>> E'en he whose heart now melts in tender lays,
>> Shall shortly want the generous tear he pays.
>> Then from his eyes thy much-loved form shall part;
>> And the last pang shall tear thee from his heart:
>> Life's idle business at one gasp be o'er,
>> The Muse forgot, and thou beloved no more.

> Here is style! How clear, how pure, proper, strong; and yet how amazingly easy! This crowns all; no stiffness, no hard words; no apparent art, no affectation; all is natural, and therefore consummately beautiful. Go thou and write likewise.
>
> (Wesley, *Works*, Vol. xiii, 417)

This passage is not at odds with what Wesley was to write eighteen years later in his *Thoughts on the Character and Writings of Mr. Prior*, for there Pope attacked is not at all for his style but for the 'exquisitely injudicious' subject and sentiment of his 'Verses to the Memory of an Unfortunate Lady'. And if it seems odd to have Prior considered as 'stiff' by contrast with Pope, he certainly is so in for instance the pindarick 'Ode to the Memory of Colonel Villiers', which Wesley singles out as one of three pieces 'which he has taken the pains to polish'. Insist as we must on the importance of Prior for the lyrical poets who came after him, there can be no question of tracing from him a 'tradition' which is an alternative to Pope's. And enthusiasts for Watts or for the Wesleys do their subjects no service at all when they set them up in competition with the greatest poet of their age.

CHRISTOPHER SMART

Fifteen years ago, in *The Late Augustans*, I proposed: 'It is not impossible that when Smart is judged over the whole range of his various production—conventional in form as well as unconventional, light and even ribald as well as devotional, urbane or tender as well as sublime—he will be thought of as the greatest English poet between Pope and Wordsworth.' In the years since, this suggestion has been treated with at best respectful incredulity; and although Smart has attracted rather more scholarly attention in the interim, I see little sign that he is now regarded otherwise than as he was then, as the author of one poem of inexplicable genius, *Song to David*, and another of fascinatingly deranged imperfection, *Jubilate Agno*. Particularly significant, and to my mind lamentable, is the decision of Dame Helen Gardner, when she assembled *A Book of Religious Verse* (1972), to follow a bad and hoary precedent in printing a mutilated version of *A Song to David*, thus denying herself space for more than one of the *Hymns and Spiritual Songs for the Festivals of the Church of England*. So far as I am concerned, my fifteen-year-old claim for Smart still stands; it awaits either vindication or rebuttal.

To my sorrow I've not been able to represent Smart 'over the whole range'. Being pressed for space, I've chosen to represent him by his secular rather than devotional pieces, selecting however for his 'divine' poem one of the *Hymns* not readily available elsewhere. Of the pieces that I give, two, it should be noted, come from the very beginning of Smart's career; his 'Morning Piece' and 'Noon Piece' appeared in a university magazine as early as 1750. And indeed it seems, to judge from these two incomparable performances, that if Smart's talent increased in power thereafter, it suffered in delicacy and refinement—as indeed one might expect, in view of the ravages which a misery, largely but not wholly self-inflicted, later subjected him to.

The achievement of 'A Morning Piece, Or an hymn for the hay-makers' (p. 87) can best be seen by comparing it with John Cunningham's 'Morning' (p. 103). Cunningham's poem is delightful: fresh, uncluttered, authenticating itself at every step as it cleaves true to one immediate experience after another. How wasteful, we rightly think, the time spent by other poets (by Cunningham himself in other poems) on invoking rhetorical or mythological figures to mediate between them and a sensed experience which ('See the chattering swallow spring;/Darting through the one-arch'd bridge') was all the time available to them in memory, if only they had stayed still long enough to attend to it! And a taste in poetry such as ours will be, if we have schooled ourselves on the post-Imagist poetry of our own time, will reasonably enough see in Cunningham's modest but solid and refreshing piece a vindication of such a post-Imagist slogan as the late William Carlos Williams's 'No ideas but in things'. This is surely a right and valuable response, so far as it goes. But to turn to Smart's poem is to move into a realm that post-Imagist poetics has never dreamed of. In 'A Morning Piece' one of the traditional rhetorical figures, *prosopopoeia* (or personification), so far from mediating between the poet and his experience, is a way of lifting that experience to a new power. By means of it, each item of sensuously registered and remembered experience becomes, while retaining its itemized integrity, a sign and manifestation of an energy abroad in the waking world. 'Strong Labour got up with his pipe in his mouth/And stoutly strode over the dale'—so misread, in his excitement, Oliver Goldsmith, adding, 'There is not a man now living who could write such a line'. And what did Goldsmith mean, if not that the real labourer smoking real tobacco in a real pipe ('He lent new perfume to the breath of the south') is also, by this way of putting it, an instance and a proof of the energy altogether more generally called 'labour' (for instance the labour of bees in the flower or the hive), of which the perfume might as readily be sweat or honey as tobacco? By contrast, John Cunningham's 'Philomel' is the merest inert short-hand for 'nightingale'.

And the proof that this indeed was Smart's vision (which is to say, his experience) is in that aspect of his writing which is least controvertible as it is least demonstrable—in his 'ear', in the sureness and promptness with which he switches rhythms. Rhythm—this is how an energy manifests itself, and when we switch rhythms we are discriminating among energies (energies abroad outside us, and within us only if we choose to invite them in, as it is the poet's glory to do). Smart's switching of rhythms, so much in contrast with Cunningham's solid trochees (themselves an achievement in a century so tuned to the iambic), was what the Pindaric ode required of its poets, as did the operatic aria. Smart's changes of gear strike me as manifestly superior to Gray's laborious and creditable attempts at the same effect, as also to such a bravura-piece as Dryden's 'Alexander's Feast', where each change of rhythm simulates the entry of a musical instrument. And Smart achieves it all without raising the key of his speech above the Horatian, 'Let us e'en talk a little like folks of this world'.

When Smart moves from his 'Morning Piece' to his 'Noon Piece', he does more than move through the hours of the forenoon. A perception announced in the 'Morning Piece' ('Sweet Society the bride . . .') is now permitted to parade in its full disconcerting grandeur: 'energies' are created or given substance by nurture as well as nature. Even before we get to 'Sidney's high-wrought stories', the allusions to pastoral convention ('Colin Clout and *Yorkshire* Will') have made us realize that 'nurture', which we might as well call 'culture', if it has not actually *produced* energies (and perhaps it has), has at all events so radically transformed energies (for instance the energies of human sexuality) that it deserves to be ranked on a level with Nature herself. And thus it is in a garden ('Where Flora's flock, by nature wild/To discipline are reconcil'd,/, And laws and order cultivate,/Quite civiliz'd into a state') that the human agents can with decency and self-respect surrender to the urgent promptings of their sexual appetites. What light this context throws back on to the ambiguous dangerousness of that salient image—'Their scythes upon the adverse bank/Glitter 'mongst th' entangled trees'—would be a study in itself. Let it be said at least that this mid-eighteenth-century pastoral escapes as certainly as seventeenth-century pastorals like Marvell's, from the socio-political reading that William Empson has found so rewarding in respect of less ambitious pastorals, like Gay's *Beggar's Opera* or Gray's *Elegy* Smart's poems claim to have a metaphysical import; their rhythms and their *prosopopoeia* claim as much; and only if the claim is granted, can those dimensions of their panoply be justified.

The ode 'To Admiral Sir George Pocock' is certainly an inferior performance, and notable more for astonishing eccentricities than for secure achievement. And yet, what extraordinary audacities there are—

> When Christ, the seaman, was aboard,
> Swift as an arrow to the *White* . . .

And in any case I could not miss the chance of showing how Smart, no less than the other distraught devotional poet Cowper, has his connections with the quite other side of eighteenth-century lyrics represented by the naval ballads.

The hymn for the day of St. Philip and St. James was chosen from among many, which deserve attention no less, chiefly for two reasons: first, 'In the choir of Christ and WREN' captures more completely than any other line in Smart's poetry what seems to have become his governing preoccupation or obsession (much complicated apparently by his having married a Papist), his wish to make St Paul's in London supplant St Peter's in Rome as the metropolitan church of Christendom; secondly, because

> And the lily smiles supremely
> Mentioned by the Lord on earth ...

merits John Middleton Murry's comment, 'This is the true, the strange Christian *naïveté*'—to which one need only add that, within the universe of poetic rhetoric, this simplicity pierces, and counts for so much, precisely because it strikes into a fabric that is not simple at all, but on the contrary elaborately patterned. The marching power of Smart's rhythms, in these hymns that he envisaged sung by massed congregations, is as evident here as in the hymn on the Nativity, or in *A Song to David* itself. And appropriate as it undoubtedly is to the full-throated unqualified celebration that Smart intended in these poems, the loss of fineness and variable flexibility since the 'Morning Piece' and 'Noon Piece' ought to be noted.

WILLIAM COWPER

On 19 November 1787 Cowper was visited by the clerk of the parish of All Saints, Northampton, who asked him to compose some verses which could be printed at the foot of the Bill of Mortality, i.e. the list which the parish clerk published each Christmas, of the parishioners who had died during the year. In a letter written eight days later Cowper described the dialogue which ensured between him and John Cox, the clerk:

> To this I replied;—'Mr. Cox, you have several men of genius in your town, why have you not applied to them? There is a namesake of yours in particular, Cox the statuary, who, everybody knows, is a first-rate maker of verses. He surely is the man of all the world for your purpose.' 'Alas! Sir, I have heretofore borrowed help from him, but he is a gentleman of so much reading that the people of our town cannot understand him.'

Accordingly Cowper composed verses not just for 1787, but also for 1788, 1789, 1790, 1792 and 1793. Each poem was published anonymously as a broadside and can thus be considered as in the strictest sense *popular* literature. The poem for 1788, with significantly an epigraph from Horace, is particularly fine.

The point of the anecdote is that Cowper was even more 'a gentleman of . . . much reading' than Mr. Cox the sculptor; but that, as a poet of genius rather than 'a first-rate maker of verses', he could, when he wanted to, write so that 'the people of our town' might understand him. This was a point of pride for Cowper, and he reverts to it often in his letters. When he undertook to translate Homer, for instance, he wanted to surpass previous translators by bringing out what he took to be the heroic plainness of Homer's language. And it should come as no surprise that Cowper, like the Wesleys, took Prior to be the model and master, for the eighteenth century, of such a plain and popular style as he needed for the Bills of Mortality, for other broadsides that he wrote, and for his hymns.

(The relationship with the Wesleys may be close. In the poem for the Bill of Mortality in 1788 appears the stanza:

> Sad waste! for which no after-thrift atones:
> The grave admits no cure of guilt or sin;
> Dew-drops may deck the turf that hides the bones,
> But tears of godly grief ne'er flow within.

And this may owe something to the mockery which six years before John Wesley had heaped on Pope's couplet from 'Verses to the Memory of an Unfortunate Lady':

> Yet shall thy grave with rising flowers be dress'd,
> And the green turf lie light upon thy breast.

'Who would not,' says Wesley, 'go to hell, to have the green turf grow upon his grave? Nay, and primroses too! For the poet assures her,—

> There the first roses of the spring shall blow!')

Cowper is a poet of very wide range indeed, and he was as much the master of elevated and florid diction as of the plain and popular. In particular, as a man with a very lively sense of humour (which he valued all the more, from being recurrently a victim of insane melancholia), Cowper in many poems—repeatedly, for instance, in *The Task*, or in that masterpiece of barely controlled hysteria, the 'Ode on the Death of Mrs. Throckmorton's Bulfinch'— exploited to comic effect the disparity between elevated diction and humble or apparently trivial subject matter, or else calculated switches and transitions from one level of diction to another. In the anthologies Cowper's achievement with these techniques inevitably, and quite properly, bulks large; the more narrowly focussed concern of this collection permits us to represent him by pieces in which he is plain and forceful. If this means that his flair for verbal comedy gets rather little showing, it brings out on the other hand his masculine trenchancy, whether he is commenting on Admiral Keppel's court-martial or on how 'God moves in a mysterious way'. Cowper uses the same straightforward, hard-hitting style, whether he is addressing his friends and neighbours as members of the same congregation, or as fellow-citizens perturbed by public affairs like the Gordon riots or the slave-trade or the war with revolutionary France.

And not only in style are the secular and the religious poems at one. For God's ways of moving are never more mysterious than when He brings about those events for which even today our lawyers can find no better explanation than to call them Acts of God; when for instance he sends the Royal George with all her complement to the bottom, not when she is in action against the enemy nor in heavy weather on the high seas, but when she seems to be securely moored by the harbour-wall; or when (to take the case never explicit in these poems but behind all or most of them) he singles out for the curse of intermittent insanity the humane and cultivated poet, who cannot avoid his doom though he withdraws from public life into a well-cushioned provincial retirement. To Cowper, a Calvinist as Watts had been, as the Wesleys very deliberately were not, this aspect of God—His omnipotence, which is to say His total freedom to act as He chooses in ways that seem to human reason unjust and unaccountable—was something borne out by every moment of waking life. The marvel is that this constant awareness did not paralyse the poet, nor did it hypnotize him so that he could not take a lively and partisan interest in the public happenings of his time.

JOHN NEWTON

There are few nowadays to whom the Reverend John Newton is even a name. And among those few there are some, I fear, for whom the name conjures up a grotesque image, both comic and horrifying, of a Pecksniffian hypocrite who walked the planks of his slave-ship in the South Atlantic, reflecting aloud, for the sake of the human cattle chained to their gratings below, 'Glorious things of thee are spoken/Zion, city of our God'; a monster of complacency who later, after a well-publicized 'conversion', harried into insanity his parishioner William Cowper, by hell-fire sermons expounding Calvinist doctrine at its most rigid and ferocious.

In fact Newton, as the captain of a slave-ship, was as humane as possible by the standards, and given the conditions, of the slave-trade in his day. His conversion was publicized, much later, precisely to give ammunition to those who wanted the slave-trade outlawed. The records of the Evangelical Movement show that, far from being an extremist, Newton continually tried to mediate between the Calvinist and the Arminian wings. And as for Cowper, he had known suicidal fits of insane melancholia before he ever met Newton, and the seeds of it were in congenital hypochondria. But all this, it will seem, is to plead no more than mitigating circumstances. By the standards of his day, both in his first profession and his second one, John Newton was temperate and enlightened—very well; but then (it will be said) the standards of his day were abominable. It is better to take the bull by the horns and admit that Newton was a remarkably simple, even an obtuse man. This at least saves him from the charge of hypocrisy. He was sincere within his limits, which were narrow.

Long before humanitarian feeling and the political genius of William Wilberforce made the slave-trade a burning issue of social morality, men like James Thomson and William Shenstone had perceived the monstrous anomaly of Sunday services at sea for the crews of slave-ships. But Newton, self-educated, represents a much less sophisticated level of society than Thomson or Shenstone or his own friend, Cowper. And for the historian, just that is his irreplaceable value. Newton on his last voyage committed to his diary his fears of an insurrection among his slaves:

> We have not been wanting in care to keep it out of their power, yet (as the best mere human precaution is insufficient to guard against everything) they had found means to provide themselves with knives and other dangerous weapons and were just ripe for mischief. So true it is that except the Lord keep the city the watchman watcheth in vain!

We find it hard to credit a simplicity which could in all good faith subscribe that last pious reflection. Yet it's just this *naïveté* which, later in Newton's life, produced his best hymns:

> The prophet's sons, in times of old,
>   Though to appearance poor,
> Were rich without possessing gold,
>   And honour'd, though obscure.
>
> In peace their daily bread they eat,
>   By honest labour earn'd;
> While daily at Elisha's feet
>   They grace and wisdom learn'd.

> The prophet's presence cheer'd their toil,
>   They watch'd the words he spoke,
> Whether they turn'd the furrow'd soil,
>   Or fell'd the spreading oak.
>
> Once, as they listened to his theme,
>   Their conference was stopp'd;
> For one beneath the yielding stream,
>   A borrow'd Axe had dropp'd.
>
> 'Alas! it was not mine,' he said
>   'How shall I make it good?'
> Elisha heard, and when he pray'd,
>   The iron swam like wood.
>
> If God, in such a small affair,
>   A miracle performs,
> It shows his condescending care
>   Of poor unworthy worms.
>
> Though kings and nations in his view
>   Are but as motes and dust,
> His eye and ear are fix'd on you,
>   Who in his mercy trust.
>
> Not one concern of ours is small,
>   If we belong to him;
> To teach us this, the Lord of all
>   Once made the iron swim.

This disconcerting *literalness* in the reading of the Christian Revelation was something that more complex and self-conscious writers like Isaac Watts and George Herbert (they were Newton's favourite poets) strove to attain by strenuous moral and artistic discipline. Those who know Newton from his logs and diaries, from his 'Authentic Narrative' (of his own conversion), from his innumerable letters, will realize that for him on the contrary this *naïveté* was natural. The absence of conscious intention and strategy, the lack of pressure and strain behind the ultimate transparency, certainly makes Newton's hymns inferior, as poems, to the poems of Herbert and the best hymns of Watts and Cowper. Yet the product speaks for itself. Its poetic virtues are minimal perhaps, yet real and rare, and moral as much as literary. For it is honesty, the refusal to slip anything over on the reader or the congregation, which pins down the miracle at its most literal, by *rhyme*:

> 'Alas! it was not mine', he said,
> 'How shall I make it good?'
> Elisha heard, and when he pray'd
> The iron swam like wood.

And it is the same wide-eyed concern to get the point home at its most astounding which justifies what seems at first sight a clear case of that bane of eighteenth-century poetry, the superfluous because 'stock' epithet:

> For one beneath the yielding stream
> A borrow'd axe had dropp'd.

It is of the nature of streams to 'yield'. This one didn't—and that's just the point; simple enough in all conscience, but in its very simplicity massively disconcerting.

The tang of colloquial idiom is everywhere in Newton:

> The Manna, favour'd Israel's meat,
>   Was gather'd day by day;
> When all the host was serv'd, the heat
>   Melted the rest away.
>
> In vain to hoard it up they try'd,
>   Against tomorrow came;
> It then bred worms and putrify'd,
>   And proved their sin and shame.
>
> 'Twas daily bread, and would not keep,
>   But must be still renew'd;
> Faith should not want a hoard or heap,
>   But trust the Lord for food.

> The truths by which the soul is fed,
>   Must thus be had afresh;
> For notions resting in the head
>   Will only feed the flesh.
>
> However true, they have no life
>   Or unction to impart;
> They breed the worms of pride and strife,
>   But cannot cheer the heart.
>
> Nor can the best experience past
>   The life of faith maintain;
> The brightest hope will faint at last,
>   Unless supply'd again.
>
> Dear Lord, while we in pray'r are found,
>   Do thou the Manna give;
> Oh! let it fall on all around,
>   That we may eat and live.

"'Twas daily bread, and would not keep . . .', 'Must thus be *had* afresh . . .'—this is the language of the eighteenth-century small shopkeeper and thrifty housewife, an idiom which has not got into English poetry at all, except through the hymn-book. Perhaps Newton's most audacious and brilliant use of the colloquial is, on an off-rhyme, at the end of 'By the poor widow's oil and meal':

> Then let not doubts your mind assail,
>   Remember God has said,
> 'The cruse and barrel shall not fail,
>   My people shall be fed.'
>
> And thus, though faint it often seems,
>   He keeps their grace alive;
> Supply'd by his refreshing streams,
>   Their dying hopes revive.
>
> Though in ourselves we have no stock,
>   The Lord is nigh to save;
> The door flies open when we knock,
>   And 'tis but ask and have.

The people who spoke this language—and John Newton who wrote for them, because he was one of them—are much stranger to us than their social betters whom we encounter in poetry so much more often. They were, for instance, much more callous, in a way which our humanitarianism finds hard to forgive, which is however easy to understand when we consider that they were only one defaulting creditor away from Gin Lane or the Debtor's Prison, only one press-gang away from the floating slums that were the British warships. They had, in any case, compensating virtues. In particular they saw piety and religious observance in terms of history which was literally true, and doctrine that was to be explained, and then accepted or rejected, not explained away or allowed to dissolve behind a mist of emotional indulgence. At their most fervent, their fervour was always related to the literally true and the doctrinally exact. As a result they produced a body of religious poetry which is the least *religiose* of any that one can think of.

MATTHEW PRIOR

On Exodus iii.14. I am that I am
An Ode

Written in 1688, as an Exercise at
St John's College, Cambridge

I

Man! Foolish Man!
Scarce know'st thou how thy self began;
Scarce hast thou Thought enough to prove Thou art;
Yet steel'd with study'd Boldness, thou dar'st try
To send thy doubting Reason's dazled Eye 5
Through the mysterious Gulph of vast Immensity.
Much thou canst there discern, much thence impart.
   Vain Wretch! suppress thy knowing Pride;
     Mortifie thy learned Lust:
Vain are thy Thoughts, while thou thy self art Dust. 10

II

Let Wit her Sails, her Oars let Wisdom lend;
The Helm let politick Experience guide:
Yet cease to hope thy short-liv'd Bark shall ride
Down spreading Fate's unnavigable Tide.
   What, tho' still it farther tend? 15
     Still 'tis farther from its End;
And in the Bosom of that boundless Sea,
Still finds its Error lengthen with its Way.

III

With daring Pride and insolent Delight
Your Doubts resolv'd you boast, your Labours crown'd;   20
And, *EUREKA!* your God, forsooth is found
Incomprehensible and Infinite.
But is He therefore found? Vain Searcher! no:
Let your imperfect Definition show,
That nothing You, the weak Definer, know.   25

IV

  Say, why shou'd the collected Main
  It self within it self contain?
Why to its Caverns shou'd it sometimes creep,
  And with delighted Silence sleep
On the lov'd Bosom of its Parents Deep?   30
  Why shou'd its num'rous Waters stay
In comely Discipline, and fair Array,
Till Winds and Tides exert their high Commands?
  Then prompt and ready to obey,
  Why do the rising Surges spread   35
Their op'ning Ranks o'er Earth's submissive Head,
Marching thro' different Paths to different Lands?

V

  Why does the constant Sun
With measur'd Steps his radiant Journeys run?
Why does He order the Diurnal Hours   40
To leave Earth's other Part, and rise in Ours?
Why does He wake the correspondent Moon,
And fill her willing Lamp with liquid Light,
Commanding Her with delegated Pow'rs
To beautifie the World, and bless the Night?   45

   Why does each animated Star
Love the just limits of it's proper Sphere?
   Why does each consenting Sign
   With prudent Harmony combine
In Turns to move, and subsequent appear,   50
To gird the Globe, and regulate the Year?

VI

Man does with dangerous Curiosity
   Those unfathom'd Wonders try:
With fancy'd Rules and arbitrary Laws
Matter and Motion he restrains;   55
And study'd Lines and fictious Circles draws:
   Then with imagin'd Soveraignty
   Lord of his new HYPOTHESIS he reigns.
He reigns: How long? 'till some Usurper rise;
And he too, mighty Thoughtful, mighty Wise,   60
Studies new Lines, and other Circles feigns.
From this last Toil again what Knowledge flows?
   Just as much, perhaps, as shows,
   That all his Predecessor's Rules
Were empty Cant, all JARGON of the Schools;   65
That he on T'other's Ruin rears his Throne;
And shows his Friend's Mistake, and thence confirms his own.

VII

On Earth, in Air, amidst the Seas and Skies,
   Mountainous Heaps of Wonders rise;
   Whose tow'ring Strength will ne'er submit   70
To Reason's Batteries, or the Mines of Wit:
Yet still enquiring, still mistaking Man,
Each Hour repuls'd, each Hour dare onward press;
And levelling at GOD his wandring Guess,

(That feeble Engine of his reasoning War, 75
Which guides his Doubts, and combats his Despair)
Laws to his Maker the learn'd Wretch can give:
Can bound that Nature, and prescribe that Will,
Whose pregnant Word did either Ocean fill:
Can tell us whence all BEINGS are, and how they move and live. 80
   Thro' either Ocean, foolish Man!
   That pregnant Word sent forth again,
Might to a World extend each ATOM there;
For every Drop call forth a Sea, a Heav'n for every Star.

VIII

Let cunning Earth her fruitful Wonders hide; 85
And only lift thy staggering Reason up
To trembling CALVARY's astonish'd Top;
Then mock thy Knowledge, and confound thy Pride,
Explaining how Perfection suffer'd Pain,
Almighty languish'd, and Eternal dy'd: 90
How by her Patient Victor Death was slain;
And Earth prophan'd, yet bless'd with Deicide.
Then down with all thy boasted Volumes, down;
   Only reserve the Sacred One:
     Low, reverently low, 95
   Make thy stubborn Knowledge bow;
Weep out thy Reason's, and thy Body's Eyes;
   Deject thy self, that Thou may'st rise;
To look to Heav'n, be blind to all below.

IX

Then Faith, for Reason's glimmering Light, shall give 100
   Her Immortal Perspective;
And Grace's Presence Nature's Loss retrieve:
Then thy enliven'd Soul shall see,

That all the Volumes of Philosophy,
With all their Comments, never cou'd invent 105
　So politick an Instrument,
To reach the Heav'n of Heav'ns, the high Abode,
Where MOSES places his Mysterious God,
As was that Ladder which old JACOB rear'd,
When Light Divine had human Darkness clear'd; 110
And his enlarg'd Ideas found the Road,
Which Faith had dictated, and Angels trod.

To a Lady:

She refusing to continue a Dispute with me, and leaving me in the Argument

An Ode

Spare, gen'rous victor, spare the slave
　Who did unequal war pursue;
That more than triumph he might have,
　In being overcome by you.

In the dispute whate'er I said, 5
　My heart was by my tongue belied;
And in my looks you might have read,
　How much I argu'd on your side.

You, far from danger as from fear
　Might have sustain'd an open fight: 10
For seldom your opinions err:
　Your eyes are always in the right.

Why, fair one, would you not rely
   On reason's force with beauty's join'd?
Could I their prevalence deny,   15
   I must at once be deaf and blind.

Alas! not hoping to subdue,
   I only to the fight aspir'd:
To keep the beauteous foe in view
   Was all the glory I desir'd.   20

But she, howe'er of vict'ry sure,
   Contemns the wreath too long delay'd;
And, arm'd with more immediate power,
   Calls cruel silence to her aid.

Deeper to wound, she shuns the fight: 25
   She drops her arms to gain the field:
Secures her conquest by her flight;
   And triumphs, when she seems to yield.

So when the Parthian turn'd his steed,
   And from the hostile camp withdrew;   30
With cruel skill the backward reed
   He sent; and as he fled, he slew.

A Better Answer to Cloe Jealous

Dear Cloe, how blubbered is that pretty face!
Thy cheek all on fire, and thy hair all uncurled.
Prithee, quit this caprice; and (as old Falstaff says)
Let us e'en talk a little like folks of this world.

How canst thou presume, thou hast leave to destroy 5
The beauties, which Venus but lent to thy keeping?
Those looks were designed to inspire love and joy:
More ord'nary eyes may serve people for weeping.

To be vext at a trifle or two that I writ,
Your judgement at once, and my passion you wrong: 10
You take that for fact, which will scarce be found wit:
'Od's life! must one swear to the truth of a song?

What I speak, my fair Cloe, and what I write, shews
The difference there is betwixt Nature and Art:
I court others in verse; but I love thee in prose: 15
And they have my whimsies; but thou hast my heart.

The God of us verse-men (you know, child) the sun
How after his journeys he sets up his rest:
If at morning o'er Earth 'tis his fancy to run,
At night he reclines on his Thetis's breast. 20

So when I am wearied with wand'ring all day,
To thee, my delight, in the evening I come;
No matter what beauties I saw in my way,
They were but my visits, but thou art my home.

Then finish, dear Cloe, this pastoral war, 25
And let us like Horace and Lydia agree:
For thou art a girl as much brighter than her
As he was a poet sublimer than me.

An Ode

The merchant, to secure his treasure,
   Conveys it in a borrow'd name:
Euphelia serves to grace my measure;
   But Cloe is my real flame.

My softest verse, my darling lyre
   Upon Euphelia's toilet lay;
When Cloe noted her desire
   That I should sing, that I should play.

My lyre I tune, my voice I raise;
   But with my numbers mix my sighs:
And whilst I sing Euphelia's praise,
   I fix my soul on Cloe's eyes.

Fair Cloe blush'd: Euphelia frown'd:
   I sung and gaz'd; I play'd and trembl'd:
And Venus to the Loves around
   Remark'd, how ill we all dissembl'd.

ANNE FINCH,
COUNTESS OF WINCHILSEA

Life's Progress

How gaily is at first begun
    Our life's uncertain race!
Whilst yet that sprightly morning sun
With which we just set out to run
    Enlightens all the place.   5

How smiling the world's prospect lies,
    How tempting to go through!
Not Canaan to the Prophet's eyes,
From Pisgah with a sweet surprise
    Did more inviting shew.   10

How promising's the book of Fate
    Till throughly understood!
Whilst partial hopes such lots create
As may the youthful fancy treat
    With all that's great and good.   15

How soft the first ideas prove,
    Which wander through our minds!
How full the joys, how free the love,
Which does that early season move
    As flowers the western winds!   20

Our sighs are then but vernal air;
  But April-drops our tears,
Which swiftly passing, all grows fair,
Whilst beauty compensates our care,
  And youth each vapour clears.   25

But oh! too soon, alas, we climb;
  Scarce feeling, we ascend
The gently rising hill of Time,
From whence with grief we see that prime,
  And all its sweetness, end.   30

The die now cast, our station known,
  Fond expectation past;
The thorns, which former days had sown,
To crops of late repentance grown,
  Through which we toil at last.   35

Whilst every care's a driving harm
  That helps to bear us down;
Which faded smiles no more can charm,
But every tear's a winter-storm,
  And every look's a frown.   40

Till with succeeding ills opprest,
  For joys we hop'd to find;
By age, too, rumpled and undrest,
We, gladly sinking down to rest,
  Leave following crowds behind.   45

A Nocturnal Reverie

In such a Night, when every louder Wind
Is to its distant Cavern safe confin'd;
And only gentle Zephyr fans his Wings,
And lonely Philomel, still waking, sings;
Or from some Tree, fam'd for the Owl's delight, 5
She, halloing clear, directs the Wand'rer right ...
In such a Night, when passing Clouds give place
Or thinly veil the Heav'ns mysterious Face;
When in some River, overhung with Green,
The waving Moon and trembling Leaves are seen ... 10
When freshen'd Grass now bears itself upright
And makes cool Banks to pleasing Rest invite,
Whence springs the Woodbind, and the Bramble-Rose,
And where the sleepy Cowslip shelter'd grows ...
Whilst now a paler Hue the Foxglove takes, 15
Yet checquers still with Red the dusky brakes ...
When scatter'd Glow-worms, but in Twilight fine,
Show trivial Beauties watch their Hour to shine
(Whilst *Salisb'ry* stands the Test of every Light,
In perfect Charms, and perfect Virtue bright) ... 20
When Odours, which declin'd repelling Day,
Thro' temp'rate Air uninterrupted stray;
When darken'd Groves their softest Shadows wear,
And falling Waters we distinctly hear;
When thro' the Gloom more venerable shows 25
Some ancient Fabrick, awful in Repose,
While Sunburnt Hills their swarthy Looks conceal
And swelling Haycocks thicken up the Vale ...
When the loos'd Horse now, as his Pasture leads,
Comes slowly grazing thro' th'adjoining Meads, 30

Whose stealing Pace, and lengthen'd Shade we fear
Till torn up Forage in his Teeth we hear . . .
When nibbling Sheep at large pursue their Food,
And unmolested Kine rechew the Cud;
When Curlews cry beneath the Village-walls,   35
And to her straggling Brood the Partridge calls . . .
Their shortliv'd Jubilee the Creatures keep,
Which but endures whilst Tyrant-Man does sleep.
  When a sedate Content the Spirit feels
And no fierce Light disturb, whilst it reveals,   40
But silent Musings urge the Mind to seek
Something too high for Syllables to speak;
Till the free Soul, to a compos'dness charm'd,
Finding the Elements of Rage disarm'd
(O'er all below a solemn Quiet grown),   45
Joys in th'inferiour World, and thinks it like her Own . . .
In such a Night let Me abroad remain,
Till Morning breaks, and All's confus'd again;
Our Cares, our Toils, our Clamours are renew'd,
Or Pleasures, seldom reach'd, again pursu'd.   50

ISAAC WATTS

To the Right Honourable
JOHN Lord CUTS
                        At the Siege
                        of *Namur*

The Hardy Soldier

I

'O why is Man so thoughtless grown?
Why guilty Souls in haste to die?
Vent'ring the leap to the Worlds unknown,
Heedless to Arms and Blood they fly.

II

Are Lives but worth a Soldier's Pay?   5
Why will ye join such wide Extremes,
And stake Immortal Souls, in play
At desperate Chance, and Bloody Games?

III

Valour's a nobler Turn of Thought,
Whose pardon'd Guilt forbids her Fears: 10
Calmly she meets the deadly Shot
Secure of Life above the Stars.

IV

But Frenzy dares eternal Fate,
And spurr'd with Honour's airy Dreams,
Flies to attack th' infernal Gate,
And force a Passage to the Flames.'

V

Thus hov'ring o'er NAMURIA's Plains,
Sung heav'nly Love in *Gabriel*'s Form:
Young THRASO felt the moving Strains,
And vow'd to pray before the Storm.

VI

Anon the thundering Trumpet calls;
Vows are but Wind, the Hero cries;
Then swears by Heav'n, and scales the Walls,
Drops in the Ditch, despairs and dies.

Few Happy Matches

I

Say, mighty Love, and teach my Song
To whom thy sweetest Joys belong,
  And who the Happy Pairs
Whose yielding Hearts, and joining Hands,
Find Blessings twisted with their Bands,
  To soften all their Cares.

II

Not the wild Herd of Nymphs and Swains
That thoughtless fly into the Chains,
   As Custom leads the Way:
If there be Bliss without Design,
Ivies and Oaks may grow and twine,
   And be as blest as they.

III

Not sordid Souls of earthy Mould
Who drawn by Kindred Charms of Gold
   To dull Embraces move:
So two rich Mountains of *Peru*
May rush to wealthy Marriage too,
   And make a World of Love.

IV

Not the mad Tribe that Hell inspires
With wanton Flames; those raging Fires
   The purer Bliss destroy:
On *Aetna*'s Top let Furies wed,
And Sheets of Lightning dress the Bed
   T'improve the burning Joy.

V

Nor the dull Pairs whose marble Forms
None of the melting Passions warms,
   Can mingle Hearts and Hands:
Logs of green Wood that quench the Coals
Are marry'd just like *Stoic* souls,
   With Osiers for their Bands.

VI

Not Minds of melancholy Strain,
Still silent, or that still complain,
  Can the dear Bondage bless:
As well may heavenly Consorts spring
From two old Lutes with ne'er a String,   35
  Or none beside the Bass.

VII

Nor can the soft Enchantments hold
Two jarring Souls of angry Mould,
  The Rugged and the Keen:
Sampson's young Foxes might as well   40
In Bonds of chearful Wedlock dwell,
  With Firebrands ty'd between.

VIII

Nor let the cruel Fetters bind
A gentle to a savage Mind;
  For Love abhors the Sight: 45
Loose the fierce Tyger from the Deer,
For native Rage and native Fear
  Rise and forbid Delight.

IX

Two kindest Souls alone must meet,
'Tis Friendship makes the Bondage sweet,   50
  And feeds their mutual Loves:
Bright *Venus* on her rolling Throne
Is drawn by gentlest Birds alone,
  And *Cupids* yoke the Doves.

Submission to Afflictive Providences

Job i.21

Naked as from the Earth we came,
    And crept to Life at first,
We to the Earth return again,
    And mingle with our Dust.

The dear Delights we here enjoy,
    And fondly call our own,
Are but short Favours borrow'd Now,
    To be repay'd Anon.

'Tis God that lifts our Comforts high,
    Or sinks 'em in the Grave.
He gives, and (blessed be his Name)
    He takes but what he gave.

Peace, all our angry Passions then,
    Let each rebellious Sigh
Be silent at his Sovereign Will,
    And every Murmur die.

If smiling Mercy crown our Lives
    Its Praises shall be spread,
And we'll adore the Justice too
    That strikes our Comforts dead.

Life the Day of Grace and Hope
Eccles. ix.4, 5, 6, 10

Life is the Time to serve the Lord,
The Time t'insure the great Reward;
And while the Lamp holds out to burn
The vilest Sinner may return.

Life is the Hour that God has giv'n
To 'scape from Hell and fly to Heav'n,
The Day of Grace, and Mortals may
Secure the Blessings of the Day.

The Living know that they must die,
But all the Dead forgotten lie;
Their Memory and their Sense is gone,
Alike unknowing and unknown.

Their Hatred and their Love is lost,
Their Envy bury'd in the Dust;
They have no Share in all that's done
Beneath the Circuit of the Sun.

Then what my thoughts design to do,
My Hands, with all your Might pursue,
Since no Device, nor Work is found,
Nor Faith, nor Hope beneath the Ground.

There are no Acts of Pardon pass'd
In the cold Grave to which we haste,
But Darkness, Death, and long Despair
Reign in Eternal Silence there.

The Passion and Exaltation of Christ

Thus saith the Ruler of the Skies,
  Awake my dreadful Sword;
Awake my Wrath, and smite the Man
  My fellow, saith the Lord.

Vengeance receiv'd the dread Command,   5
  And armed down she flys,
Jesus submits t'his Father's Hand,
  And bows his Head and dies.

But oh! the Wisdom and the Grace
  That join with Vengeance now!   10
He dies to save our Guilty Race,
  And yet he rises too.

A Person so divine was he
  Who yielded to be slain,
That he could give his Soul away,   15
  And take his Life again.

Live, glorious Lord, and reign on high,
  Let every Nation sing,
And Angels sound with endless Joy
  The Saviour and the King.   20

Look on him whom they pierced, and mourn

Infinite Grief! amazing Woe!
   Behold my bleeding Lord:
Hell and the Jews conspir'd his Death,
   And us'd the Roman Sword.

Oh the sharp Pangs of smarting Pain 5
   My dear Redeemer bore,
When knotty Whips, and ragged Thorns
   His sacred Body tore!

But knotty Whips and ragged Thorns
   In vain do I accuse, 10
In vain I blame the Roman Bands,
   And the more spightful Jews.

'Twere you, my Sins, my cruel Sins,
   His chief Tormentors were;
Each of my Crimes became a Nail, 15
   And Unbelief the Spear,

'Twere you that pull'd the Vengeance down,
   Upon his guiltless Head:
Break, break my Heart, oh burst mine Eyes,
   And let my Sorrows bleed. 20

Strike, mighty Grace, my flinty Soul
   Till melting Waters flow,
And deep Repentance drown mine Eyes
   In undissembled Woe.

Crucifixion to the World by the Cross of Christ

Gal. vi.14

When I survey the wond'rous Cross
Where the young Prince of Glory dy'd,
My richest Gain I count but Loss,
And pour Contempt on all my Pride.

Forbid it, Lord, that I should boast
Save in the Death of Christ my God;
All the vain things that charm me most,
I sacrifice them to his Blood.

See from his Head, his Hands, his Feet,
Sorrow and Love flow mingled down;
Did e'er such Love and Sorrow meet?
Or Thorns compose so rich a Crown?

His dying Crimson like a Robe
Spreads o'er his Body on the Tree,
Then am I dead to all the Globe,
And all the Globe is dead to me.

Were the whole Realm of Nature mine,
That were a present far too small;
Love so amazing, so divine
Demand my Soul, my Life, my All.

A Prospect of Heaven makes Death easy

There is a Land of pure Delight
   Where Saints Immortal reign;
Infinite Day excludes the Night,
   And Pleasures banish Pain.

There everlasting Spring abides, 5
   And never-withering Flowers:
Death like a narrow Sea divides
   This Heav'nly Land from ours.

Sweet Fields beyond the swelling Flood
   Stand drest in living Green: 10
So to the Jews Old Canaan stood,
   While Jordan roll'd between.

But timorous Mortals start and shrink
   To cross this narrow Sea,
And linger shivering on the Brink, 15
   And fear to launch away.

O could we make our Doubts remove,
   These gloomy Doubts that rise,
And see the Canaan that we love,
   With unbeclouded Eyes, 20

Could we but climb where Moses stood,
   And view the Landskip o'er,
Not Jordan's Stream, nor Death's cold Flood
   Should fright us from the Shore.

The Church the Garden of Christ
Sol. Song 4.12, 14, 15. and 5.1

We are a Garden wall'd around,
Chosen and made peculiar Ground;
A little Spot inclos'd by Grace
Out of the World's wide Wilderness.

Like Trees of Myrrh and Spice we stand, 5
Planted by God the Father's Hand;
And all his Springs in Sion flow,
To make the young Plantation grow.

Awake, O heavenly Wind, and come,
Blow on this Garden of Perfume; 10
Spirit Divine, descend and breathe
A gracious Gale on Plants beneath.

Make our best Spices flow abroad
To entertain our Saviour-God:
And faith, and Love, and Joy appear, 15
And every Grace be active here.

Let my Beloved come, and taste
His pleasant Fruits at his own Feast.
I come, my Spouse, I come, he crys,
With Love and Pleasure in his Eyes. 20

Our Lord into his Garden comes,
Well pleas'd to smell our poor Perfumes,
And calls us to a Feast divine,
Sweeter than Honey, Milk, or Wine.

Eat of the Tree of Life, my Friends, 25
The Blessings that my Father sends;
Your Taste shall all my Dainties prove,
And drink abundance of my Love.

Jesus, we will frequent thy Board,
And sing the Bounties of our Lord: 30
But the rich Food on which we live
Demands more Praise than Tongues can give.

Miracles at the Birth of Christ

The King of Glory sends his Son
To make his Entrance on this Earth;
Behold the Midnight bright as Noon,
And Heav'nly Hosts declare his Birth.

About the young Redeemer's Head 5
What Wonders and what Glories meet!
An unknown Star arose, and led
The Eastern Sages to his Feet.

Simeon and Anna both conspire
The Infant-Saviour to proclaim, 10
Inward they felt the sacred Fire,
And bless'd the Babe, and own'd his Name.

Let Jews and Greeks blaspheme aloud,
And treat the holy Child with scorn;
Our Souls adore th'Eternal God 15
Who condescended to be born.

Hosanna to Christ

Hosanna to the Royal Son
   Of David's antient line!
His natures two, his person one,
   Mysterious and divine.

The Root of David, here, we find,   5
   And Off-spring, are the same:
Eternity and time are join'd
   In our Immanuel's name.

Blest he that comes to wretched man,
   With peaceful news from Heav'n!   10
Hosannas, of the highest strain,
   To Christ the Lord be giv'n.

Should we, dear Lord, refuse to take
   Th'Hosanna on our tongues,
The rocks and stones would rise and break   15
   Their silence into songs.

The Shortness and Misery of Life

  Our Days, alas! our Mortal Days
    Are short and wretched too;
  Evil and Few the Patriarch says,
    And well the Patriarch knew.

'Tis but at best a narrow Bound
   That Heaven allows to Men,
And Pains and Sins run thro' the Round
   Of threescore Years and ten.

Well, if ye must be sad and few,
   Run on, my Days, in haste.
Moments of Sin, and Months of Woe,
   Ye cannot fly too fast.

Let Heavenly Love prepare my Soul,
   And call her to the Skies,
Where Years of long Salvation roll,
   And Glory never dies.

ANON

Admiral Benbow

O, we sail'd to Virginia, and thence to Fayal,
Where we water'd our shipping, and then we weigh'd all;
Then in view on the seas, boys, seven sail we did espy;
O, we manned our capstan, and weigh'd speedily.

Now the first we came up with was a brigantine sloop, 5
And we asked if the others were big as they look'd;
But turning to windward as near as we could lie,
We found there was ten men-o'-war acruizing thereby.

O! we drew up our squadron in a very nice line,
And boldly we fought them for full four hours' time; 10
Then the day being spent, boys, and the night coming on,
We let them alone till the very next morn.

The very next morn the engagement prov'd hot,
And brave Admiral Benbow receiv'd a chain shot;
And when he was wounded, to his men he did say, 15
'Take me up in your arms, boys, and carry me away.'

O! the guns they did rattle, and the bullets did fly,
But Admiral Benbow for help would not cry:
'Take me down to the cockpit, there is ease for my smarts,
If my merry men see me it will sure break their hearts.' 20

And there Captain Kirby proved a coward at last,
And with Wade played at bo-peep behind the mainmast;
And there they did stand, boys, and shiver and shake,
For fear that those French dogs their lives they should take.

The very next morning at the break of day   25
They hoisted their topsails and so bore away.
We bore up for Port Royal, where the people flocked much
To see Admiral Benbow carried to Kingston Church.

Come all you brave fellows, wherever you've been,
Let us drink to the health of our King and our Queen,   30
And another good health to the girls that we know,
And a third for remembrance of brave Admiral Benbow.

The Duke of Ormond's Health

Neptune frown, and *Boreas* roar,
   Let thy Thunder bellow;
Noble ORMOND'S now come o'er,
   With each gallant *English* fellow:
      Then to welcome him ashore   5
      To his Health a brimmer pour,
   Till every one be mellow,
   Remembring *Rodondello*, remembring *Rodondello*,
   Remembring, remembring *Rodondello*,
   Remembring, remembring *Rodondello*.   10

Tho' at *Cales* they scap'd our Guns,
   By strong wall'd umbrello:
Civil Jarrs and Plundring Dons,
   Curse upon the metal yellow:

    Had the valiant Duke more Men,   15
    He a Victor there had been,
As late at *Rodondello*,
As late, &c.

Mounsieur and Petite *Anjou*,
  Plot your state Intrigo: 20
Take new Marshall *Chateaurenault*,
  Then consult with *Spanish Deigo*:
    And new Glory to advance
    Sing *Te Deum* through all France,
Pour la Victoire at Vigo,   25
Pour la, &c.

We mean while to crown our Joy,
  Laughing at such folly,
To their Health full Bowls employ,
  Who have cur'd our Melancholy: 30
    And done more to furnish Tales
    Now at *Vigo*, then at *Cales*
Fam'd *Essex* did, or *Rawleigh*,
Brave *Essex*, &c.

Great *Eliza* on the Main,   35
  Quell'd the Dons Boastado;
In Queen ANN'S Auspicious Reign,
  Valour conquers, not Bravado:
    Come but such another Year,
    We the spacious Sea shall clear,   40
Of *French* and *Spain*'s Armado
Of *French*, &c.

Once more then tho' *Boreas* roar,
  And loud Thunder bellow;
Since Great ORMOND is come o'er,   45

With each gallant *English* fellow:
    Let us welcome all a Shore,
    To each Health a brimmer pour,
  Till everyone be mellow,
  Remembring *Rodondello*, &c.   50

JOSEPH ADDISON

Ode

The spacious firmament on high
With all the blue ethereal sky,
And spangled heavens, a shining frame,
Their great Original proclaim:
The unwearied sun, from day to day, 5
Does his Creator's power display,
And publishes to every land
The work of an almighty hand.

Soon as the evening shades prevail,
The moon takes up the wondrous tale, 10
And nightly to the listening earth
Repeats the story of her birth:
Whilst all the stars that round her burn,
And all the planets in their turn,
Confirm the tidings as they roll, 15
And spread the truth from pole to pole.

What though, in solemn silence, all
Move round the dark, terrestrial ball?
What though nor real voice nor sound
Amid their radiant orbs be found? 20

In reason's ear they all rejoice,
And utter forth a glorious voice,
For ever singing, as they shine,
'The hand that made us is divine'.

JOHN GAY

Sweet William's Farewell to Black-Eyed Susan
A Ballad

All in the Downs the fleet was moor'd,
    The streamers waving in the wind,
When black-eyed Susan came aboard:
    'Oh! where shall I my true love find?
Tell me, ye jovial sailors, tell me true,   5
If my sweet William sails among the crew.'

William, who high upon the yard
    Rock'd with the billow to and fro,
Soon as her well-known voice he heard,
    He sigh'd and cast his eyes below: 10
The cord slides swiftly through his glowing hands
And (quick as lightning) on the deck he stands.

So the sweet lark, high-pois'd in air,
    Shuts close his pinions to his breast
(If, chance, his mate's shrill call he hear)   15
    And drops at once into her nest.
The noblest captain in the British fleet
Might envy William's lips those kisses sweet.

'Oh! Susan, Susan, lovely dear,
    My vows shall ever true remain;
Let me kiss off that falling tear,
    We only meet to part again.
Change, as ye list, ye winds; my heart shall be
The faithful compass that still points to thee.

Believe not what the landsmen say,
    Who tempt with doubts thy constant mind:
They'll tell thee sailors, when away,
    In every port a mistress find.
Yes, yes, believe them when they tell thee so,
For thou art present wheresoe'er I go.

If to far India's coast we sail,
    Thy eyes are seen in diamonds bright;
Thy breath is Afric's spicy gale,
    Thy skin is ivory, so white.
Thus every beauteous object that I view
Wakes in my soul some charm of lovely Sue.

Though battle call me from thy arms,
    Let not my pretty Susan mourn;
Though cannons roar, yet safe from harms
    William shall to his dear return.
Love turns aside the balls that round me fly,
Lest precious tears should drop from Susan's eye.'

The boatswain gave the dreadful word,
    The sails their swelling bosom spread;
No longer must she stay aboard:
    They kiss'd, she sigh'd, he hung his head;
Her lessening boat unwilling rows to land:
'Adieu!' she cries; and wav'd her lily hand.

Polyphemus' Song

    I rage, I melt, I burn,
The feeble god has stabb'd me to the heart.
    Thou trusty pine,
Prop of my god-like steps, I lay thee by.
Bring me a hundred reeds, of decent growth,   5
To make a pipe for my capacious mouth;
In soft enchanting accents let me breathe
Sweet Galatea's beauty, and my love.

    O ruddier than the cherry!
    O sweeter than the berry!   10
    O nymph more bright
    Than moonshine night,
Like kidlings blithe and merry!
Ripe as the melting cluster!
No lily has such lustre;   15
    Yet hard to tame
    As raging flame,
And fierce as storms that bluster!

Songs from The Beggar's Opera

I

        If any wench Venus's girdle wear,
           Though she be never so ugly,
        Lillies and roses will quickly appear,
           And her face looks wondr'ous smuggly.
        Beneath the left ear, so fit but a cord,   5
           (A rope so charming a Zone is!)
        The youth in his cart hath the air of a lord,
           And we cry, There dies an Adonis!

II

        Were I laid on Greenland's coast,
           And in my arms embrac'd my lass;
        Warm amidst eternal frost,
           Too soon the half year's night would pass.
Polly.   Were I sold on Indian soil,   5
           Soon as the burning day was clos'd,
        I could mock the sultry toil,
           When on my charmer's breast repos'd.
Macheath. And I would love you all the day,
Polly.   Every night would kiss and play,   10
Macheath. If with me you'd fondly stray
Polly.   Over the hills and far away.

III

        Youth's the season made for joys,
           Love is then our duty;
        She alone who that employs,
           Well deserves her beauty.

    Let's be gay,   5
     While we may,
   Beauty's a flower despis'd in decay.

Chorus. Youth's the season, &c.

   Let us drink and sport to-day,
    Ours is not to-morrow.   10
   Love with youth flies swift away,
    Age is nought but sorrow.
     Dance and sing,
     Time's on the wing,
   Life never knows the return of spring. 15

Chorus. Let us drink, &c.

IV

   Thus when the Swallow, seeking prey,
    Within the sash is closely pent,
   His consort with bemoaning lay,
    Without sits pining for th'event.
  Her chatt'ring lovers all around her skim; 5
  She heeds them not (poor bird) her soul's with him.

RICHARD GLOVER

Admiral Hosier's Ghost

As near Porto-Bello lying
  On the gently swelling flood,
At midnight, with streamers flying,
  Our triumphant navy rode;
There while Vernon sat all-glorious   5
  From the Spaniards' late defeat,
And his crews, with shouts victorious,
  Drank success to England's fleet;

On a sudden, shrilly sounding,
  Hideous yells and shrieks were heard;   10
Then, each heart with fear confounding,
  A sad troop of ghosts appear'd,
All in dreary hammocks shrouded,
  Which for winding-sheets they wore,
And, with looks by sorrow clouded,   15
  Frowning on that hostile shore.

On them gleam'd the moon's wan lustre,
  When the shade of Hosier brave
His pale bands was seen to muster,
  Rising from their watery grave: 20
O'er the glimmering wave he hied him,

Where the Burford rear'd her sail,
With three thousand ghosts beside him,
  And in groans did Vernon hail.

'Heed, O heed, our fatal story, 25
  I am Hosier's injur'd ghost;
You, who now have purchas'd glory
  At this place where I was lost,
Though in Porto-Bello's ruin
  You now triumph, free from fears, 30
When you think on our undoing,
  You will mix your joy with tears.

See these mournful spectres, sweeping
  Ghastly o'er this hated wave,
Whose wan cheeks are stain'd with weeping; 35
  These were English captains brave;
Mark those numbers, pale and horrid,
  Those were once my sailors bold,
Lo, each hangs his drooping forehead,
  While his dismal tale is told. 40

I, by twenty sail attended,
  Did this Spanish town affright;
Nothing then its wealth defended
  But my orders not to fight;
O! that in this rolling ocean 45
  I had cast them with disdain,
And obey'd my heart's warm motion
  To have quelled the pride of Spain.

For resistance I could fear none,
  But with twenty ships had done 50
What thou, brave and happy Vernon,
  Hast achiev'd with six alone.

Then the Bastimentos never
  Had our foul dishonour seen,
Nor the sea the sad receiver
  Of this gallant train had been.

Thus, like thee, proud Spain dismaying,
  And her galleons leading home,
Though, condemn'd for disobeying,
  I had met a traitor's doom,
To have fallen, my country crying
  'He has play'd an English part,'
Had been better far than dying
  Of a griev'd and broken heart.

Unrepining at thy glory,
  Thy successful arms we hail;
But remember our sad story,
  And let Hosier's wrongs prevail.
Sent in this foul clime to languish,
  Think what thousands fell in vain,
Wasted with disease and anguish,
  Not in glorious battle slain.

Hence with all my train attending
  From their oozy tombs below,
Through the hoary foam ascending,
  Here I feed my constant woe;
Here, the Bastimentos viewing,
  We recall our shameful doom,
And, our plaintive cries renewing,
  Wander through the midnight gloom.

O'er these waves, for ever mourning,
  Shall we roam depriv'd of rest,
If to Britain's shores returning
  You neglect my just request:

After this proud foe subduing, 85
   When your patriot friends you see,
Think on vengeance for my ruin,
   And for England sham'd in me.'

HENRY CAREY

A Loyal Song

Sung at the Theatres

God save great George our King,
Long live our noble King;
   God save the King.
Send him victorious,
Happy and glorious, 5
Long to reign over us;
   God save the King.

O Lord our God arise,
Scatter his enemies,
   And make them fall. 10
Confound their politicks,
Frustrate their knavish tricks;
On him our hopes we fix;
   O, save us all.

Thy choicest gifts in store 15
On George be pleased to pour;
   Long may he reign.
May he defend our laws,
And ever give us cause
To say with heart and voice, 20
   God save the King.

He comes, he comes . . .

He comes, he comes, the hero comes,
Sound your trumpets, beat your drums;
From port to port let cannons roar
His welcome to the British shore.

Prepare, prepare, your songs prepare; 5
Loudly rend the echoing air;
From pole to pole your joys resound,
For virtue is with glory crown'd.

CHARLES WESLEY

He comes! he comes! the Judge severe...

He comes! he comes! the Judge severe,
The seventh trumpet speaks him near;
His lightnings flash, his thunders roll,
How welcome to the faithful soul!

From heaven angelic voices sound,
See the almighty Jesus crowned,
Girt with omnipotence and grace!
And glory decks the Saviour's face.

Descending on his azure throne,
He claims the kingdom for his own;
The kingdoms all obey his word,
And hail him their triumphant Lord.

Shout, all the people of the sky,
And all the saints of the Most High!
Our Lord, who now his right obtains,
For ever and for ever reigns.

Captain of Israel's Host and Guide

Exodus xiii

Captain of Israel's host, and guide
  Of all who seek the land above,
Beneath thy shadow we abide,
  The cloud of thy protecting love;
Our strength, thy grace; our rule, thy word; 5
Our end, the glory of the Lord.

By thine unerring Spirit led,
  We shall not in the desert stray;
We shall not full direction need,
  Nor miss our providential way; 10
As far from danger as from fear,
While love, almighty love, is near.

O Thou Eternal Victim slain

O Thou Eternal Victim slain,
A sacrifice for guilty man,
By the Eternal Spirit made
An offering in the sinner's stead;
Our everlasting Priest art thou, 5
And plead'st Thy Death for sinners now.

Thy Offering still continues new,
The vesture keeps its bloody hue,

Thou stand'st the ever-slaughter'd Lamb,
Thy Priesthood still remains the same,   10
Thy years, O God, can never fail,
Thy goodness is unchangeable.

O that our faith may never move,
But stand unshaken as thy love!
Sure evidence of things unseen,   15
Now let it pass the years between,
And view thee bleeding on the Tree,
My God, Who dies for me, for me.

Wrestling Jacob

Come, O thou Traveller unknown,
  Whom still I hold, but cannot see,
My company before is gone,
  And I am left alone with thee,
With thee all night I mean to stay,   5
And wrestle till the break of day.

I need not tell thee who I am,
  My misery, or sin declare,
Thyself hast called me by my name,
  Look on thy hands, and read it there,   10
But who, I ask thee, who art thou?
Tell my thy name, and tell me now.

In vain thou strugglest to get free,
  I never will unloose my hold:

Art thou the Man that died for me? 15
   The secret of thy love unfold,
Wrestling I will not let thee go,
Till I thy name, thy nature know.

Wilt thou not yet to me reveal
   Thy new, unutterable name? 20
Tell me, I still beseech thee, tell;
   To know it now resolved I am,
Wrestling I will not let thee go,
Till I thy name, thy nature know.

'Tis all in vain to hold thy tongue, 25
   Or touch the hollow of my thigh:
Though every sinew be unstrung,
   Out of my arms thou shalt not fly.
Wrestling I will not let thee go,
Till I thy name, thy nature know. 30

What though my shrinking flesh complain,
   And murmur to contend so long,
I rise superior to my pain,
   When I am weak then I am strong,
And when my all of strength shall fail, 35
I shall with the God-Man prevail.

My strength is gone, my nature dies,
   I sink beneath thy weighty hand,
Faint to revive, and fall to rise;
   I fall, and yet by faith I stand, 40
I stand, and will not let thee go,
Till I thy name, thy nature know.

Yield to me now—for I am weak;
   But confident in self-despair:

Speak to my heart, in blessings speak, 45
   Be conquered by my instant prayer,
Speak, or thou never hence shalt move,
And tell me, if thy name is Love.

'Tis Love, 'tis Love! Thou died'st for me,
   I hear thy whisper in my heart. 50
The morning breaks, the shadows flee:
   Pure Universal Love thou art;
To me, to all, thy bowels move,
Thy nature and thy name is Love.

My prayer hath power with God; the Grace 55
   Unspeakable I now receive,
Through Faith I see thee face to face,
   I see thee face to face, and live:
In vain I have not wept, and strove,
Thy nature and thy name is Love. 60

I know thee, Saviour, who thou art,
   Jesus, the feeble sinner's friend;
Nor wilt thou with the night depart,
   But stay, and love me to the end;
Thy mercies never shall remove, 65
Thy nature and thy name is Love.

The Sun of Righteousness on me
   Hath rose with healing in his wings,
Withered my nature's strength; from thee
   My soul its life and succour brings, 70
My help is all laid up above;
Thy nature and thy name is Love.

Contented now upon my thigh
   I halt, till life's short journey end;

All helplessness, all weakness I, 75
   On thee alone for strength depend,
Nor have I power, from thee, to move;
Thy nature and thy name is Love.

Lame as I am, I take the prey,
   Hell, earth, and sin with ease o'ercome; 80
I leap for joy, pursue my way,
   And as a bounding hart fly home,
Through all eternity to prove
Thy nature and thy name is Love.

JAMES THOMSON

Rule Britannia!

When Britain first, at Heaven's command,
   Arose from out the azure main,
This was the charter of the land,
   And guardian angels sung this strain:
     'Rule, Britannia, rule the waves;
     Britons never will be slaves.'

The nations, not so blest as thee
   Must, in their turns, to tyrants fall;
While thou shalt flourish great and free,
   The dread and envy of them all.
     'Rule' &c.

Still more majestic shalt thou rise,
   More dreadful from each foreign stroke;
As the loud blast that tears the skies
   Serves but to root thy native oak.
     'Rule' &c.

Thee haughty tyrants ne'er shall tame;
   All their attempts to bend thee down
Will but arouse thy generous flame,
   But work their woe, and thy renown.
     'Rule' &c.

To thee belongs the rural reign;
  Thy cities shall with commerce shine;
All thine shall be the subject main;
  And every shore it circles, thine.   25
    'Rule' &c.

The Muses, still with freedom found,
  Shall to thy happy coast repair:
Blest isle! with matchless beauty crowned,
  And manly hearts to guard the fair: 30
    'Rule, Britannia, rule the waves,
    Britons never will be slaves.'

WILLIAM COLLINS

Ode on the Death of Thomson

In yonder grave a druid lies,
   Where slowly winds the stealing wave!
The year's best sweets shall duteous rise
   To deck its Poet's sylvan grave!

In yon deep bed of whispering reeds 5
   His airy harp shall now be laid,
That he, whose heart in sorrow bleeds,
   May love through life the soothing shade.

Then maids and youths shall linger here,
   And while its sounds at distance swell, 10
Shall sadly seem in Pity's ear
   To hear the woodland pilgrim's knell.

Remembrance oft shall haunt the shore
   When Thames in summer wreaths is drest,
And oft suspend the dashing oar 15
   To bid his gentle spirit rest!

And oft as ease and health retire
   To breezy lawn, or forest deep,
The friend shall view yon whitening spire,
   And 'mid the varied landscape weep. 20

But thou, who own'st that earthy bed,
   Ah! what will every dirge avail?
Or tears, which love and pity shed,
   That mourn beneath the gliding sail?

Yet lives there one, whose heedless eye   25
   Shall scorn thy pale shrine glimmering near?
With him, sweet bard, may fancy die,
   And joy desert the blooming year.

But thou, lorn stream, whose sullen tide
   No sedge-crown'd sisters now attend,   30
Now waft me from the green hill's side,
   Whose cold turf hides the buried friend!

And see, the fairy valleys fade,
   Dun night has veil'd the solemn view!
Yet once again, dear parted shade,   35
   Meek Nature's child, again adieu!

The genial meads assign'd to bless
   Thy life, shall mourn thy early doom;
Their hinds, and shepherd girls shall dress
   With simple hands thy rural tomb.   40

Long, long, thy stone, and pointed clay
   Shall melt the musing Briton's eyes.
O! vales, and wild woods, shall he say,
   In yonder grave your Druid lies!

PHILIP DODDRIDGE

Meditations on the Sepulchre in the Garden

John xix.41

The Sepulchres, how thick they stand
Thro' all the Road on either Hand!
And burst upon the startling Sight
In ev'ry Garden of Delight!

Thither the winding Alleys tend; 5
There all the flow'ry Borders end;
And Forms, that charm'd the Eyes before,
Fragrance, and Musick are no more.

Deep in that damp and silent Cell
My Fathers, and my Brethren dwell; 10
Beneath its broad and gloomy Shade
My Kindred, and my Friends are laid.

But, while I tread the solemn Way,
My Faith that Saviour would survey,
Who deign'd to sojourn in the Tomb, 15
And left behind a rich Perfume.

My thoughts with Extacy unknown,
While from his Grave they view his Throne,
Thro' mine own Sepulchre can see
A Paradise reserv'd for me. 20

God's delivering Goodness acknowledged and trusted

2 Cor. i.10

A Song for the 5th of November

Praise to the Lord, whose mighty Hand
So oft revealed hath saved our Land;
And, when united Nations rose,
Hath sham'd and scourg'd our haughtiest Foes.

When mighty Navies from afar   5
To *Britain* wafted floating War,
His Breath dispers'd them all with Ease,
And sunk their Terror in the Seas.

While for our Princes they prepare
In Caverns deep a burning Snare;   10
He shot from Heav'n a piercing Ray,
And the dark Treach'ry brought to Day.

Princes and Priests again combine
New Chains to forge, new Snares to twine;
Again our gracious God appears,   15
And breaks their Chains, and cuts their Snares.

Obedient Winds at his Command
Convey his *Hero* to our Land;
And sons of *Rome* with Terror view
And Speed their Flight, when none persue.   20

Such great Deliv'rance God hath wrought,
And down to us Salvation brought;
And still the Care of Guardian-Heav'n
Secures the Bliss itself hath giv'n.

In Thee we trust, Almighty Lord, 25
Continu'd Rescue to afford:
Still be thy pow'rful Arm made bare,
For all thy Servants Hopes are there.

CHRISTOPHER SMART

A Morning Piece,
Or an hymn for the hay-makers

Quin etiam Gallum noctem explaudentibus aliis
Auroram clara consuetum voce vocare.
         Lucret.

Brisk Chanticleer his matins had begun,
 And broke the silence of the night.
And thrice he call'd aloud the tardy sun,
 And thrice he hail'd the dawn's ambiguous light;
Back to their graves the fear-begotten phantoms run. 5

 Strong Labour got up.—With his pipe in his mouth
  He stoutly strode over the dale,
 He lent new perfume to the breath of the south,
  On his back hung his wallet and flail.
Behind him came Health from her cottage of thatch, 10
Where never physician had lifted the latch.

First of the village Colin was awake,
And thus he sung reclining on his rake.
  Now the rural graces three
  Dance beneath yon maple tree; 15
  First the vestal Virtue, known
  By her adamantine zone;
  Next to her in rosy pride,
  Sweet Society the bride;

      Last Honesty, full seemly drest   20
        In her cleanly home-spun vest.
The abbey bells in wak'ning rounds
      The warning peal have giv'n;
And pious Gratitude resounds
      Her morning hymn to heav'n.   25

All nature wakes—the birds unlock their throats,
And mock the shepherd's rustic notes.
    All alive o'er the lawn,
    Full glad of the dawn,
      The little lambkins play,   30
Sylvia and Sol arise,—and all is day—
    Come, my mates, let us work,
    And all hands to the fork,
While the Sun shines, our hay-cocks to make.
    So fine is the day,   35
      And so fragrant the hay,
That the meadow's as blith as the wake.

    Our voices let's raise
    In Phoebus's praise,
Inspir'd by so glorious a theme.   40
    Our musical words
    Shall be join'd by the birds,
And we'll dance to the tune of the stream

A Noon-Piece,
Or the Mowers at Dinner

> Jam pastor umbras cum grege languido,
> Rivumque fessus quaerit, & horridi
>   Dumeta Silvani, caretque
>   Ripa vagis taciturna ventis.
> Hor.

The Sun is now too radiant to behold,
And vehement he sheds his liquid rays of gold:
  No cloud appears thro' all the wide expanse;
    And short, but yet distinct, and clear,
The mimic shadows dance.   5

    Fat Mirth, and Gallantry the gay,
    And romping Ecstasy 'gin play.
    Now myriads of young Cupids rise,
    And open all their joy-bright eyes,
    Filling with infant prate the grove,   10
    And lisp in sweetly-fault'ring love.
    In the middle of the ring,
    Mad with May, and wild of wing,
    Fire-ey'd Wantonness shall sing.

    By the rivulet on the rushes,   15
    Beneath a canopy of bushes
    Where the ever-faithful *Tray*
    Guards the dumplings and the whey,
    Collin Clout and *Yorkshire* Will
    From the leathern flasket swill.   20

Their scythes upon the adverse bank
   Glitter 'mongst th'entangled trees,
Where the hazles form a rank,
   And court'sy to the courting breeze.

Ah! Harriet! sovereign mistress of my heart, 25
   Could I thee to these meads decoy,
New grace to each fair object thou'dst impart,
   And heighten ev'ry scene to perfect joy.

   On a bank of fragrant thyme,
   Beneath yon stately, shadowy pine, 30
   We'll with the well-disguised hook
   Cheat the tenants of the brook;
   Or where coy Daphne's thickest shade
   Drives amorous Phoebus from the glade,
   There read Sidney's high-wrought stories 35
   Of ladies charms, and heroes glories;
   Thence fir'd, the sweet narration act,
   And kiss the fiction into fact.

Or satiate with Nature's random scenes,
Let's to the gardens regulated greens, 40
   Where Taste and Elegance command
   Art to lend her daedal hand,
   Where Flora's flock, by nature wild,
   To discipline are reconcil'd,
   And laws and order cultivate, 45
   Quite civiliz'd into a state.

   From the Sun and from the show'r,
   Haste we to yon boxen bow'r,
   Secluded from the teizing pry
   Of Argus curiosity: 50
   There, while Phoebus' golden mean,

The gay meridian, is seen,
E'er decays the lamp of light,
And length'ning shades stretch out to night—
Seize, seize the hint—each hour improve
(This is morality in love)
Lend, lend thine hand—O let me view
Thy parting breasts, sweet avenue!
Then,—then thy lips, the coral cell
Where all th'ambrosial kisses dwell! 60
Thus we'll each sultry noon employ
In day-dreams of ecstatic joy.

Ode to Admiral Sir George Pocock

1.

When Christ, the seaman, was aboard,
   Swift as an arrow to the *White*,
While Ocean his rude rapture roar'd,
   The vessel gain'd the Haven with delight:
We therefore first to him the song renew, 5
Then sing of Pocock's praise, and make the point in view.

2.

The Muse must humble e're she rise,
   And kneel to kiss her Master's feet,
Thence at one spring she mounts the skies
   And in New Salem vindicates her seat; 10
Seeks to the temple of th'Angelick choir,
And hoists the English flag upon the topmost spire.

3.

O Blessed of the Lord of Hosts,
 In either India most renown'd,
The Echo of the Eastern coasts, 15
 And all th'Atlantic shore thy name resound.—
The victor's clemency, the seaman's art,
The cool delib'rate head, the warm undaunted heart.

4.

My pray'r was with thee, when thou sail'd
 With prophecies of sure success; 20
My thanks to Heav'n that thou prevail'd
 Shall last as long as I can breathe or bless;
And built upon thy deeds my song shall tow'r,
And swell, as it ascends, in spirit and in pow'r.

5.

There is no thunder half so loud, 25
 As God's applauses in the height,
For those, that have his name avow'd,
 Ev'n *Christian* patriots valorous and great;
Who for the general welfare stand or fall,
And have no sense of self, and know no dread at all. 30

6.

Amongst the numbers lately fir'd
 To act upon th'heroic plan,
Grace has no worthier chief inspir'd
 Than that sublime, insuperable man,
Who could th'outnumb'ring French so oft defeat, 35
And from th'HAVANNAH stor'd his brave victorious fleet.

7.

And yet how silent his return
　With scarce a welcome to his place—
Stupidity and unconcern
　Were settled in each voice and on each face.　　40
As private as myself he walk'd along,
Unfavour'd by a friend, unfollow'd by the throng.

8.

Thy triumph, therefore, is not here,
　Thy glories for a while postpon'd,
The hero shines not in his sphere,　　45
　But where the Author of all worth is own'd.—
Where *Patience* still persists to praise and pray
For all the Lord bestows, and all he *takes away*.

9.

Nor HOWARD, FROBISHER, or DRAKE,
　Or VERNON'S fam'd *Herculean* deed;　　50
Not all the miracles of BLAKE,
　Can the great Chart of thine exploits exceed.—
Then rest upon thyself and dwell secure,
And cultivate the arts, and feed th'*increasing* poor.

10.

O Name accustom'd and inur'd　　55
　To fame and hardship round the globe,
For which fair Honour has insur'd
　The warrior's truncheon, and the consul's robe;
Who still, the more is *done* and *understood*,
Art easy of access, and affable and good.　　60

11.

O Name acknowledged and rever'd
   Where Isis plays her pleasant stream,
Whene'er thy tale is read or heard,
   The good shall bless thee and the wise esteem;
And they, whose offspring lately felt thy care,   65
Shall IN TEN THOUSAND CHURCHES make their daily
   pray'r.

12.

'Connubial bliss and homefelt joy,
   And ev'ry social praise be thine;
Plant thou the oak, the poor employ;
   Or plans of vast benevolence design;   70
And speed, when Christ his servant shall release,
From triumph over death to everlasting peace.'

Hymn XIII
St. Philip and St. James

Now the winds are all composure,
   But the breath upon the bloom,
Blowing sweet o'er each inclosure
   Grateful off'rings of perfume.

Tansy, calaminth and daisies   5
   On the river's margin thrive;
And accompany the mazes
   Of the stream that leaps alive.

Muse, accordant to the season,
  Give the numbers life and air;   10
When the sounds and objects reason
  In behalf of praise and pray'r.

All the scenes of nature quicken,
  By the genial spirit fann'd;
And the painted beauties thicken   15
  Colour'd by the master's hand.

Earth her vigour repossessing
  As the blasts are held in ward;
Blessing heap'd and press'd on blessing,
  Yield the measure of the Lord.   20

Beeches, without order seemly,
  Shade the flow'rs of annual birth,
And the lily smiles supremely
  Mention'd by the Lord on earth.

Couslips seize upon the fallow,   25
  And the cardamine in white,
Where the corn-flow'rs join the mallow,
  Joy and health, and thrift unite.

Study sits beneath her arbour,
  By the bason's glossy side;   30
While the boat from out its harbour
  Exercise and pleasure guide.

Pray'r and praise be mine employment,
  Without grudging or regret,
Lasting life, and long enjoyment,   35
  Are not here, and are not yet.

Hark! aloud, the black-bird whistles,
   With surrounding fragrance blest,
And the goldfinch in the thistles
   Makes provision for her nest.   40

Ev'n the hornet hives his honey,
   Bluecap builds his stately dome,
And the rocks supply the coney
   With a fortress and an home.

But the servants of their Saviour,   45
   Which with gospel peace are shod,
Have no bed but what the paviour
   Makes them in the porch of God.

O thou house that hold'st the charter
   Of salvation from on high,   50
Fraught with prophet, saint, and martyr,
   Born to weep, to starve and die!

Great to-day thy song and rapture
   In the choir of Christ and WREN
When two prizes were the capture   55
   Of the hand that fish'd for men.

To the man of quick compliance
   Jesus call'd, and Philip came;
And began to make alliance
   For his master's cause and name.   60

James, of title most illustrious,
   Brother of the Lord, allow'd;
In the vineyard how industrious,
   Nor by years nor hardship bow'd!

Each accepted in his trial, 65
    One the CHEERFUL, one the JUST;
Both of love and self-denial,
    Both of everlasting trust.

Living they dispens'd salvation,
    Heav'n-endow'd with grace and pow'r; 70
And they dy'd in imitation
    Of their Saviour's final hour,

Who, for cruel traitors pleading,
    Triumph'd in his parting breath;
O'er all miracles preceding 75
    His inestimable death.

DAVID GARRICK

Hearts of Oak

Come cheer up my lads, 'tis to glory we steer,
To add something new to this wonderful year;
To honour we call you, not press you like slaves,
For who are so free as the sons of the waves?

Hearts of Oak are our ships, Hearts of Oak are our men, 5
    We always are ready,
    Steady, boys, steady,
We'll fight and we'll conquer again and again.

We ne'er meet our foes but we wish them to stay,
They ne'er meet us but they wish us away; 10
If they run, then we follow, and drive them ashore,
For if they won't fight us, we cannot do more.
              Hearts of Oak, &c.

Monsieur Thurot in the absence of Boyce
Went over to Ireland to brag the dear boys; 15
Near Man, Elliot met him, and gave him a blow,
Which sent him to tell it to Pluto below.
              Hearts of Oak, &c.

They talk to invade us, these terrible foes,
They frighten our women, our children, and beaux; 20
But if their flat bottoms in darkness come o'er,
Some Britons they'll find to receive them on shore.
              Hearts of Oak, &c.

We'll make them to run, and we'll make them to sweat,
In spite of the Devil and Russel's Gazette; 25
Then cheer up my lads, with one heart let us sing,
Our soldiers, our sailors, our statesmen, our king.
                    Hearts of Oak, &c.

JOHN WIGNELL

Neptune's Resignation

The wat'ry god, great Neptune, lay,
In dalliance soft and amorous play
   On Amphitrite's breast;
When Uproar rear'd its horrid head,
The tritons shrunk, the nereids fled,   5
   And all their fear confess'd.

Loud thunder shook the vast domain,
The liquid world was wrapp'd in flame;
   The god, amazed, spoke—
'Ye Winds, go forth and make it known   10
Who dares to shake my coral throne,
   And fill my realms with smoke.'

The Winds, obsequious, at his word
Sprung strongly up t'obey their lord,
   And saw two fleets aweigh—   15
One, victorious Hawke, was thine,
The other, Conflans' wretched line—
   In terror and dismay.

Appall'd, they view Britannia's sons
Deal death and slaughter from their guns,   20
   And strike the dreadful blow,

Which caused ill-fated Gallic slaves
To find a tomb in briny waves,
   And sink to shades below.

With speed they fly and tell their chief   25
That France was ruin'd past relief,
   And Hawke triumphant rode.
'Hawke!' cried the Fair; 'Pray who is he
That dare usurp this power at sea,
   And thus insult a god?'   30

The Winds reply—'In distant lands
There reigns a king who Hawke commands,
   He scorns all foreign force;
And when his floating castles roll
From sea to sea, from pole to pole,   35
   Great Hawke directs their course.

Or when his winged bullets fly
To punish fraud and perfidy,
   Or scourge a guilty land;
Then gallant Hawke, serenely great,   40
Though death and horror round him wait,
   Performs his dread command.'

Neptune, with wonder, heard the story
Of George's sway and Britain's glory,
   Which time shall ne'er subdue;   45
Boscawen's deeds, and Saunders' fame,
Join'd with brave Wolfe's immortal name,—
   Then cried, 'Can this be true?—

A king! he sure must be a god,
Who has such heroes at his nod 50
　To govern earth and sea:
I yield my trident and my crown
A tribute due to such renown,—
　Great George shall rule for me.'

JOHN CUNNINGHAM

Morning

In the barn the tenant cock,
   Close to partlet perch'd on high,
Briskly crows (the shepherd's clock!)
   Jocund that the morning's nigh.

Swiftly from the mountain's brow
   Shadows, nurs'd by night, retire:
And the peeping sunbeam now
   Paints with gold the village spire.

Philomel forsakes the thorn,
   Plaintive where she prates at night;
And the lark, to meet the morn,
   Soars beyond the shepherd's sight.

From the low-roof'd cottage ridge
   See the chattering swallow spring;
Darting through the one-arch'd bridge
   Quick she dips her dappled wing.

Now the pine-tree's waving top
   Gently greets the morning gale:
Kidlings, now, begin to crop
   Daisies on the dewy dale.

From the balmy sweets uncloy'd,
   (Restless till her task be done)
Now the busy bee's employ'd
   Sipping dew before the sun.

Trickling through the crevic'd rock,
   Where the limpid stream distils,
Sweet refreshment waits the flock,
   When 'tis sun-drove from the hills.

Colin's for the promis'd corn
   (Ere the harvest hopes are ripe)
Anxious; whilst the huntsman's horn,
   Boldly sounding, drowns his pipe.

Sweet, O sweet, the warbling throng,
   On the white emblossom'd spray!
Nature's universal song
   Echoes to the rising day.

AUGUSTUS TOPLADY

A Living and Dying Prayer for the Holiest Believer in the World

Rock of Ages, cleft for me,
Let me hide myself in Thee!
Let the Water and the Blood,
From thy riven Side which flow'd,
Be of Sin the double Cure, 5
Cleanse me from its Guilt and Pow'r.

Not the Labours of my Hands
Can fulfil thy Law's demands:
Could my Zeal no respite know,
Could my Tears for ever flow, 10
All for Sin could not atone:
Thou must save, and Thou alone!

Nothing in my Hand I bring;
Simply to thy Cross I cling;
Naked, come to Thee for Dress; 15
Helpless, look to Thee for Grace;
Foul, I to the Fountain fly:
Wash me, Saviour, or I die!

Whilst I draw this fleeting Breath—
When my Eye-strings break in Death— 20
When I soar through tracts unknown—
See Thee on thy Judgment-Throne—
Rock of Ages, cleft for me,
Let me hide myself in THEE!

JOHN NEWTON

Zion, or the City of God

Glorious things of thee are spoken,
   Zion, city of our God;
He whose word cannot be broken
   Formed thee for his own abode.
On the Rock of ages founded,
   What can shake thy sure repose?
With salvation's walls surrounded,
   Thou may'st smile at all thy foes.

See, the streams of living waters,
   Springing from eternal love,
Well supply thy sons and daughters,
   And all fear of want remove.
Who can faint while such a river
   Ever flows their thirst to assuage:
Grace which, like the Lord the giver,
   Never fails from age to age?

Round each habitation hovering,
   See the cloud and fire appear
For a glory and a covering,
   Showing that the Lord is near.
Thus deriving from their banner
   Light by night and shade by day,
Safe they feed upon the Manna
   Which he gives them when they pray.

Blest inhabitants of Zion, 25
    Wash'd in the Redeemer's blood!
Jesus, whom their souls rely on,
    Makes them kings and priests to God:
'Tis his love his people raises
    Over self to reign as kings, 30
And as priests, his solemn praises
    Each for a thank-off'ring brings.

Saviour, if of Zion's city
    I through grace a member am,
Let the world deride or pity, 35
    I will glory in thy name.
Fading is the worldling's pleasure,
    All his boasted pomp and show;
Solid joys and lasting treasure
    None but Zion's children know. 40

WILLIAM COWPER

This ev'ning, Delia, you and I

This ev'ning, Delia, you and I
Have manag'd most delightfully,
   For with a frown we parted;
Having contrived some trifle that
We both may be much troubled at,   5
   And sadly disconcerted.

Yet well as each perform'd their part,
We might perceive it was but art,
   And that we both intended
To sacrifice a little ease   10
For all such pretty flaws as these
   Are made but to be mended.

You knew, Dissembler! all the while
How sweet it was to reconcile
   After this heavy pelt;   15
That we should gain by this allay
When next we met, and laugh away
   The care we never felt.

Happy! when we but seek t'endure
A little pain, then find a cure   20
   By double joy requited;
For friendship, like a sever'd bone,
Improves and joins a stronger tone
   When aptly reunited.

Light Shining out of Darkness

God moves in a mysterious way,
   His wonders to perform;
He plants his footsteps in the sea,
   And rides upon the storm.

Deep in unfathomable mines
   Of never failing skill
He treasures up his bright designs,
   And works his sovereign will.

Ye fearful saints, fresh courage take:
   The clouds ye so much dread
Are big with mercy, and shall break
   In blessings on your head.

Judge not the Lord by feeble sense,
   But trust him for his grace;
Behind a frowning providence
   He hides a smiling face.

His purposes will ripen fast,
   Unfolding ev'ry hour;
The bud may have a bitter taste,
   But sweet will be the flow'r.

Blind unbelief is sure to err,
   And scan his work in vain;
God is his own interpreter,
   And he will make it plain.

Welcome Cross

'Tis my happiness below
Not to live without the cross;
But the Saviour's pow'r to know,
Sanctifying ev'ry loss.
Trials must and will befall;
But with humble faith to see
Love inscrib'd upon them all,
This is happiness to me.

God, in Israel, sows the seeds
Of affliction, pain, and toil;
These spring up, and choke the weeds
Which would else o'erspread the soil.
Trials make the promise sweet,
Trials give new life to pray'r;
Trials bring me to his feet,
Lay me low, and keep me there.

Did I meet no trials here,
No chastisement by the way,
Might I not, with reason, fear
I should prove a cast-away?
Bastards may escape the rod,
Sunk in earthly, vain delight;
But the true-born child of God
Must not, would not if he might.

Self-Acquaintance

Dear Lord, accept a sinful heart,
   Which of itself complains
And mourns, with much and frequent smart,
   The evil it contains.

There fiery seeds of anger lurk,
   Which often hurt my frame
And wait but for the tempter's work
   To fan them to a flame.

Legality holds out a bribe
   To purchase life from thee;
And discontent would fain prescribe
   How thou shalt deal with me.

While unbelief withstands thy grace,
   And puts the mercy by,
Presumption, with a brow of brass,
   Says, 'Give me, or I die.'

How eager are my thoughts to roam
   In quest of what they love!
But ah! when duty calls them home,
   How heavily they move!

Oh, cleanse me in a Saviour's blood,
   Transform me by thy pow'r,
And make me thy belov'd abode,
   And let me rove no more.

The Shrubbery

Written in a Time of Affliction

Oh, happy shades—to me unblest!
   Friendly to peace, but not to me!
How ill the scene that offers rest,
   And heart that cannot rest, agree!

This glassy stream, that spreading pine,   5
   Those alders quiv'ring to the breeze,
Might sooth a soul less hurt than mine,
   And please, if any thing could please.

But fix'd unalterable care
   Foregoes not what she feels within,   10
Shows the same sadness ev'ry where,
   And slights the season and the scene.

For all that pleas'd in wood or lawn,
   While peace possess'd these silent bow'rs,
Her animating smile withdrawn,   15
   Has lost its beauties and its pow'rs.

The saint or moralist should tread
   This moss-grown alley, musing, slow;
They seek, like me, the secret shade,
   But not, like me, to nourish woe!   20

Me fruitful scenes and prospects waste
   Alike admonish not to roam;
These tell me of enjoyments past,
   And those of sorrows yet to come.

On the Trial of Admiral Keppel

Keppel, returning from afar
  With laurels on his brow,
Comes home to wage a sharper war,
  And with a fiercer foe.

The blow was rais'd with cruel aim,
  And meant to pierce his heart,
But lighting on his well earn'd fame
  Struck an immortal part.

Slander and Envy strive to tear
  His wreath so justly won,
But Truth, who made his cause her care,
  Has bound it faster on.

The charge, that was design'd to sound
  The signal of disgrace,
Has only call'd a navy round
  To praise him to his face.

The Modern Patriot

Rebellion is my theme all day;
  I only wish 'twould come
(As who knows but perhaps it may?)
  A little nearer home.

Yon roaring boys, who rave and fight 5
  On t'other side th'Atlantic,
I always held them in the right,
  But most so when most frantic.

When lawless mobs insult the court,
  That man shall be my toast, 10
If breaking windows be the sport,
  Who bravely breaks the most.

But oh! for him my fancy culls
  The choicest flow'rs she bears,
Who constitutionally pulls 15
  Your house about your ears.

Such civil broils are my delight;
  Though some folk can't endure 'em,
Who say the mob are mad outright,
  And that a rope must cure 'em. 20

A rope! I wish we patriots had
  Such strings for all who need 'em—
What! hang a man for going mad?
  Then farewell British freedom.

Joy and Peace in Believing

Sometimes a light surprizes
  The Christian while he sings;
It is the Lord who rises
  With healing in his wings.

When comforts are declining,
   He grants the soul again
A season of clear shining
   To cheer it after rain.

In holy contemplation
   We sweetly then pursue
The theme of God's salvation,
   And find it ever new.
Set free from present sorrow,
   We cheerfully can say,
'E'en let th'unknown to-morrow
   Bring with it what it may.

It can bring with it nothing
   But he will bear us thro';
Who gives the lilies clothing
   Will clothe his people too.
Beneath the spreading heavens,
   No creature but is fed;
And he who feeds the ravens
   Will give his children bread.

Though vine, nor fig-tree neither,
   Their wonted fruit should bear,
Tho' all the field should wither,
   Nor flocks, nor herds, be there,
Yet God the same abiding,
   His praise shall tune my voice;
For while in him confiding,
   I cannot but rejoice.'

Jehovah our Righteousness

Jer. xxiii.6

My God, how perfect are thy ways!
    But mine polluted are;
Sin twines itself about my praise,
    And slides into my pray'r.

When I would speak what thou hast done
    To save me from my sin,
I cannot make thy mercies known
    But self-applause creeps in.

Divine desire, that holy flame
    Thy grace creates in me,
Alas! impatience is its name
    When it returns to thee.

This heart, a fountain of vile thoughts,
    How does it overflow,
While self upon the surface floats
    Still bubbling from below?

Let others in the gaudy dress
    Of fancied merit shine;
The Lord shall be my righteousness;
    The Lord for ever mine.

Exhortation to Prayer

What various hindrances we meet
In coming to a mercy-seat!
Yet who that knows the worth of pray'r
But wishes to be often there?

Pray'r makes the dark'ned cloud withdraw, 5
Pray'r climbs the ladder Jacob saw,
Gives exercise to faith and love,
Brings ev'ry blessing from above.

Restraining pray'r, we cease to fight;
Pray'r makes the Christian's armour bright; 10
And Satan trembles, when he sees
The weakest saint upon his knees.

While Moses stood with arms spread wide,
Success was found on Israel's side;
But when thro' weariness they fail'd, 15
That moment Amalek prevail'd.

Have you no words? Ah, think again!
Words flow apace when you complain
And fill your fellow-creature's ear
With the sad tale of all your care. 20

Were half the breath thus vainly spent,
To heav'n in supplication sent,
Your cheerful song would oft'ner be:
'Hear what the Lord has done for me!'

Prayer for Patience

Lord, who hast suffer'd all for me,
My peace and pardon to procure,
The lighter cross I bear for thee
Help me with patience to endure.

The storm of loud repining, hush.
I would in humble silence mourn;
Why should th'unburnt, tho' burning, bush
Be angry as the crackling thorn?

Man should not faint at thy rebuke,
Like Joshua falling on his face
When the curst thing that Achan took
Brought Israel into just disgrace.

Perhaps some golden wedge suppress'd,
Some secret sin, offends my God;
Perhaps that Babylonish vest,
Self-righteousness, provokes the rod.

Ah! were I buffeted all day,
Mock'd, crown'd with thorns, and spit upon,
I yet should have no right to say:
'My great distress is mine alone.'

Let me not angrily declare
No pain was ever sharp like mine;
Nor murmur at the cross I bear,
But rather weep, rememb'ring thine.

Welcome to the Table

This is the feast of heav'nly wine,
    And God invites to sup;
The juices of the living vine
    Were press'd, to fill the cup.

Oh, bless the Saviour, ye that eat,
    With royal dainties fed;
Not heav'n affords a costlier treat,
    For Jesus is the bread!

The vile, the lost, he calls to them:
    'Ye trembling souls, appear!
The righteous in their own esteem
    Have no acceptance here.

Approach, ye poor, nor dare refuse
    The banquet spread for you!'
'Dear Saviour, this is welcome news.
    Then I may venture too.'

If guilt and sin afford a plea,
    And may obtain a place,
Surely the Lord will welcome me,
    And I shall see his face!

Love Constraining to Obedience

No strength of Nature can suffice
   To serve the Lord aright;
And what she has, she misapplies
   For want of clearer light.

How long beneath the law I lay
   In bondage and distress!
I toil'd the precept to obey,
   But toil'd without success.

Then to abstain from outward sin
   Was more than I could do;
Now, if I feel its pow'r within,
   I feel I hate it too.

Then all my servile works were done
   A righteousness to raise;
Now, freely chosen in the Son,
   I freely choose his ways.

'What shall I do,' was then the word,
   'That I may worthier grow?'
'What shall I render to the Lord?'
   Is my enquiry now.

To see the Law by Christ fulfill'd,
   And hear his pard'ning voice,
Changes a slave into a child,
   And duty into choice.

The Valley of the Shadow of Death

My soul is sad and much dismay'd;
See, Lord, what legions of my foes,
With fierce Apollyon at their head,
My heav'nly pilgrimage oppose!

See, from the ever-burning lake 5
How like a smoky cloud they rise!
With horrid blasts my soul they shake,
With storms of blasphemies and lies.

Their fiery arrows reach the mark,
My throbbing heart with anguish tear; 10
Each lights upon a kindred spark,
And finds abundant fuel there.

I hate the thought that wrongs the Lord.
Oh, I would drive it from my breast
With thy own sharp two-edged sword, 15
Far as the east is from the west.

Come then, and chase the cruel host,
Heal the deep wounds I have receiv'd!
Nor let the pow'rs of darkness boast
That I am foil'd, and thou art griev'd! 20

The Negro's Complaint

To the tune of Hosiers Ghost

Forc'd from home, and all its pleasures,
    Afric's coast I left forlorn;
To increase a stranger's treasures,
    O'er the raging billows borne.
Men from England bought and sold me,   5
    Paid my price in paltry gold;
But, though theirs they have enroll'd me,
    Minds are never to be sold.

Still in thought as free as ever,
    What are England's rights, I ask,   10
Me from my delights to sever,
    Me to torture, me to task?
Fleecy locks, and black complexion
    Cannot forfeit nature's claim;
Skins may differ, but affection   15
    Dwells in white and black the same.

Why did all-creating Nature
    Make the plant for which we toil?
Sighs must fan it, tears must water,
    Sweat of ours must dress the soil.   20
Think, ye masters, iron-hearted,
    Lolling at your jovial boards;
Think how many blacks have smarted
    For the sweets your cane affords.

Is there, as ye sometimes tell us,   25
    Is there one who reigns on high?

Has he bid you buy and sell us,
   Speaking from his throne the sky?
Ask him, if your knotted scourges,
   Fetters, blood-extorting screws,   30
Are the means which duty urges
   Agents of his will to use?

Hark! he answers,—Wild tornadoes,
   Strewing yonder sea with wrecks;
Wasting towns, plantations, meadows,   35
   Are the voice with which he speaks.
He, foreseeing what vexations
   Afric's sons should undergo,
Fix'd their tyrants' habitations
   Where his whirlwinds answer—No.   40

By our blood in Afric wasted,
   Ere our necks receiv'd the chain;
By the mis'ries we have tasted,
   Crossing in your barks the main;
By our suff'rings since ye brought us   45
   To the man-degrading mart;
All sustain'd by patience taught us
   Only by a broken heart:

Deem our nation brutes no longer
   Till some reason ye shall find   50
Worthier of regard and stronger
   Than the colour of our kind.
Slaves of gold, whose sordid dealings
   Tarnish all your boasted pow'rs,
Prove that you have human feelings   55
   Ere you proudly question ours!

Sweet Meat has Sour Sauce

or, The Slave-trader in the Dumps

A trader I am to the African shore,
But since that my trading is like to be o'er
I'll sing you a song that you ne'er heard before,
        Which nobody can deny, deny,
        Which nobody can deny.

When I first heard the news it gave me a shock,
Much like what they call an electrical knock,
And now I am going to sell off my stock
        Which nobody, &c.

'Tis a curious assortment of dainty regales,
To tickle the negroes with when the ship sails,
Fine chains for the neck, and a cat with nine tails,
        Which nobody, &c.

Here's supple-jack plenty, and store of rat-tan,
That will wind itself round the sides of a man,
As close as a hoop round a bucket or can,
        Which nobody, &c.

Here's padlocks and bolts, and screws for the thumbs,
That squeeze them so lovingly till the blood comes,
They sweeten the temper like comfits or plums,
        Which nobody, &c.

When a negro his head from his victuals withdraws,
And clenches his teeth and thrusts out his paws,
Here's a notable engine to open his jaws,
        Which nobody, &c.

Thus going to market, we kindly prepare
A pretty black cargo of African ware,
For what they must meet with when they get there,
        Which nobody, &c.

'Twould do your heart good to see 'em below   30
Lie flat on their backs all the way as we go,
Like sprats on a gridiron, scores in a row,
        Which nobody, &c.

But ah! if in vain I have studied an art
So gainful to me, all boasting apart,   35
I think it will break my compassionate heart
        Which nobody, &c.

For oh! how it enters my soul like an awl!
This pity, which some people self-pity call,
Is sure the most heart-piercing pity of all,   40
        Which nobody, &c.

So this is my song, as I told you before;
Come buy off my stock, for I must no more
Carry Caesars and Pompeys to Sugar-cane shore,
        Which nobody can deny, deny,   45
        Which nobody can deny.

A Good Song

Tune: 'How happy could I be with either'

Here's a health to honest JOHN BULL,
    When he's gone we shan't find such another;
And with hearts and with glasses brim full,
    Here's a health to OLD ENGLAND his mother.

She gave him a good education,　　　　　　　　　5
　　Bade him keep to his church and his KING;
Be loyal and true to the Nation,
　　And then go be merry and sing.

Now *John* is a good humoured fellow,
　　Industrious, honest, and brave;　　　　　　10
Not afraid of his *betters* when mellow,
　　For *betters* he knows he must have.

For there must be fine lords and fine ladies,
　　There must be some *little* and *great*;
Their wealth the supply of the trade is,　　　15
　　Our hands the support of their state.

Some are born for the court and the city,
　　And some for the village and cot;
But oh! 'twere a dolorous ditty
　　If all became equal in lot.　　　　　　　　20

If our ships have no pilots to steer,
　　What wou'd 'come of poor Jack in the shrouds?
Or our troops no commanders to fear,
　　They'd soon be arm'd robbers in crouds.

Then the plough and the loom must stand still,　25
　　If they made of us *gentlemen* all;
Or all clodhoppers; then who wou'd fill
　　The parliament, pulpit, and hall?

'Rights of Man' make a very fine sound,
　　'Equal Riches' a plausible tale;　　　　　　30
But whose labour wou'd then till the ground?
　　All wou'd drink, but who'd brew the best ale?

When half naked, half starv'd in the street,
   We were wand'ring about *sans culottes*,
Wou'd *equality* go fetch us meat?   35
   Or wou'd *liberty* lengthen our coats?

That knaves are for levelling no wonder,
   'Tis easy to guess at their views;
'Tis *they* who get all by their plunder
   'Tis *they* who have nothing to lose.   40

Then away with such nonsense and stuff,
   Full of treason, confusion and blood;
Ev'ry BRITON has freedom enough
   To be *happy* as long as he's *good*.

To be rul'd by a merciful KING,   45
   To be guarded by juries and laws;
And when our work's finish'd to sing—
   This, this is true liberty's cause.

Then holloo boys! holloo boys! ever;
   For just such a nation are we;   50
'Tis our pleasure; O may it cease never!
   'Tis our pride, to be *loyal* and *free*.

To Mary

   The twentieth year is well-nigh past,
   Since first our sky was overcast;
   Ah would that this might be the last!
                My Mary!

Thy spirits have a fainter flow,
I see thee daily weaker grow—
'Twas my distress that brought thee low,
        My Mary!

Thy needles, once a shining store,
For my sake restless heretofore,
Now rust disus'd, and shine no more,
        My Mary!

For though thou gladly wouldst fulfil
The same kind office for me still,
Thy sight now seconds not thy will,
        My Mary!

But well thou play'd'st the housewife's part,
And all thy threads with magic art
Have wound themselves about this heart,
        My Mary!

Thy indistinct expressions seem
Like language utter'd in a dream;
Yet me they charm, whate'er the theme,
        My Mary!

Thy silver locks, once auburn bright,
Are still more lovely in my sight
Than golden beams of orient light,
        My Mary!

For could I view nor them nor thee,
What sight worth seeing could I see?
The sun would rise in vain for me,
        My Mary!

Partakers of the sad decline,
Thy hands their little force resign;
Yet, gently prest, press gently mine, 35
           My Mary!

And then I feel that still I hold
A richer store ten thousandfold
Than misers fancy in their gold,
           My Mary! 40

Such feebleness of limbs thou prov'st,
That now at every step thou mov'st
Upheld by two; yet still thou lov'st,
           My Mary!

And still to love, though prest with ill, 45
In wintry age to feel no chill,
With me is to be lovely still,
           My Mary!

But ah! by constant heed I know,
How oft the sadness that I show 50
Transforms thy smiles to looks of woe,
           My Mary!

And should my future lot be cast
With much resemblance of the past,
Thy worn-out heart will break at last,
           My Mary!

EOGHAN RUADH O SUILLEBHAIN

Rodney's Glory

Give ear, ye British hearts of gold,
That e'er disdain to be controlled,
Good news to you I will unfold,
   'Tis of brave Rodney's glory,
Who always bore a noble heart,   5
And from his colours ne'er would start,
But always took his country's part
Against each foe who dared t'oppose
Or blast the bloom of England's Rose,
   So now observe my story.   10

'Twas in the year of Eighty Two,
The Frenchmen know full well 'tis true,
Brave Rodney did their fleet subdue,
   Not far from old Fort Royal.
Full early by the morning's light,   15
The proud De Grasse appeared in sight,
And thought brave Rodney to affright,
With colours spread at each mast-head,
Long pendants, too, both white and red,
   A signal for engagement.   20

Our Admiral then he gave command,
That each should at his station stand,
'Now, for the sake of Old England,
   We'll show them British valour.'

Then we the British flag displayed, 25
No tortures could our hearts invade,
Both sides began to cannonade,
Their mighty shot we valued not,
We plied our 'Irish pills' so hot,
   Which put them in confusion. 30

This made the Frenchmen to combine,
And draw their shipping in a line,
To sink our fleet was their design,
   But they were far mistaken;
Broadside for broadside we let fly, 35
Till they in hundreds bleeding lie,
The seas were all of crimson dye,
Full deep we stood in human blood,
Surrounded by a scarlet flood,
   But still we fought courageous. 40

So loud our cannons that the roar
Re'echoed round the Indian shore,
Both ships and rigging suffered sore,
   We kept such constant firing;
Our guns did roar, and smoke did rise, 45
And clouds of sulphur veiled the skies,
Which filled De Grasse with wild surprise;
Both Rodney's guns and Paddy's sons
Make echo shake where'er they come,
   They fear no French or Spaniards. 50

From morning's dawn to fall of night,
We did maintain this bloody fight,
Being still regardless of their might,
   We fought like Irish heroes.
Though on the deck did bleeding lie 55
Many of our men in agony,

We resolved to conquer or die,
To gain the glorious victory,
And would rather suffer to sink or die
    Than offer to surrender. 60

So well our quarters we maintained,
Five captured ships we have obtained,
And thousands of their men were slain
    During this hot engagement;
Our British metal flew like hail, 65
Until at length the French turned tail,
Drew in their colours and made sail
In deep distress, as you may guess,
And when they got in readiness
    They sailed down to Fort Royal. 70

Now may prosperity attend
Brave Rodney and his Irishmen,
And may he never want a friend
    While he shall reign commander;
Success to our Irish officers, 75
Seamen bold and jolly tars,
Who like darling sons of Mars
Take delight in the fight
And vindicate bold England's right
    And die for Erin's glory. 80

PRINCE HOARE

The Arethusa

Come all ye jolly Sailors bold
Whose hearts are cast in honour's mould,
While England's glory I unfold:
    Huzza to the Arethusa!
She is a Frigate tight and brave
As ever stemm'd the dashing wave;
    Her men are staunch
    To their fav'rite Launch,
And when the foe shall meet our fire,
Sooner than strike we'll all expire
    On board of the Arethusa.

'Twas with the spring-fleet she went out,
The English Channel to cruize about,
When four French sail, in show so stout,
    Bore down on the Arethusa.
The fam'd Belle Poule straight ahead did lie.
The Arethusa seem'd to fly;
    Not a sheet, or a Tack
    Or a brace did she slack,
Tho' the Frenchmen laugh'd, and thought it stuff,
But they knew not the handful of men, how tough,
    On board of the Arethusa.

On deck five hundred men did dance,
The stoutest they could find in France;
We, with two hundred, did advance 25
    On board of the Arethusa.
Our captain hail'd the Frenchman, 'Ho!'
The Frenchman cry'd out, 'Hallo!'
    'Bear down, d'ye see,
    To our Admiral's lee.' 30
'No, no,' says the Frenchman, 'that can't be.'
'Then I must lug you along with me,'
    Says the saucy Arethusa.

The fight was off the Frenchman's land.
We forc'd them back upon their strand; 35
For we fought till not a stick would stand
    Of the gallant Arethusa.
And now we've driven the foe ashore,
Never to fight with Britons more,
    Let each fill a glass 40
    To his favorite lass!
A health to our Captain, and Officers true,
And all that belong to the jovial crew
    On board of the Arethusa!

HENRY PHIPPS, EARL OF MULGRAVE

'Our line was form'd'

I

Our line was form'd, the French lay to,
   One sigh I gave to Poll on shore,
Too cold I thought our last adieu—
Our parting kisses seem'd too few,
   If we should meet no more. 5
But love, avast! my heart is Oak,
   Howe's daring signal floats on high;
I see through roaring cannon's smoke
Their awful line subdu'd and broke.
   They strike! they sink, they fly! 10

Chorus.
Now (danger past) we'll drink and joke,
Sing 'Rule Britannia', 'Hearts of Oak!'
And toast before each Martial tune—
'Howe, and the Glorious First of June!'

II

My limb struck off, let soothing art 15
   The chance of war to Poll explain;
Proud of the loss, I feel no smart
But as it wrings my Polly's heart
   With sympathetic pain.

Yet she will think (with love so tried)   20
   Each scar a beauty on my face,
And as I strut with martial pride
On timber toe by Polly's side,
   Will call my limp a grace.

III

Farewell to every sea delight: 25
   To cruize with eager watchful days,
The skilful chace by glim'ring night,
The well-worked ship, the gallant fight,
   The lov'd Commander's praise.
Yet Polly's love and constancy   30
   With prattling babes more joy shall bring,
Proud when my boys shall first at sea
Follow great Howe to Victory,
   And serve our noble King.

WILLIAM BLAKE

Song

How sweet I roam'd from field to field
And tasted all the summer's pride,
Till I the prince of love beheld
Who in the sunny beams did glide!

He shew'd me lilies for my hair,
And blushing roses for my brow;
He led me through his gardens fair
Where all his golden pleasures grow.

With sweet May dews my wings were wet,
And Phoebus fir'd my vocal rage;
He caught me in his silken net,
And shut me in his golden cage.

He loves to sit and hear me sing,
Then, laughing, sports and plays with me;
Then stretches out my golden wing,
And mocks my loss of liberty.

COMMENTARY AND NOTES

MATTHEW PRIOR

LIFE

Matthew Prior, born 1664 to humble nonconformist parents, was taken up by the Earl of Dorset, who sent him to Westminster School and Cambridge. Loyal to James II while he was on the throne, Prior was taken unawares by the Revolution. But his satirical abilities won him entry to a diplomatic career, first in the Whig interest in Holland and France negotiating a treaty with the French. After 1700, back in England, he deserted the Whigs and associated with Swift and the Tories. It was they who sent him again to Paris (1711–1713) to negotiate the end of another war. Trapped with the rest of the Tory administration by Queen Anne's death in 1713, he came home to two years' not very onerous imprisonment (1715–1717). Released, he was much cherished through his last years by the Tory ex-minister Harley, whom under questioning he had refused to incriminate. He died in 1721.

p. 1 On Exodus iii.14

The text is from H. B. Wright and M. K. Spears (eds.) *The Literary Works of Matthew Prior* (2nd ed., Oxford, 1971).

Exodus iii.14 reads: 'And God said unto Moses, I AM THAT I AM: and he said, Thus shalt thou say unto the children of Israel, I AM hath sent me unto you.'

Though the poem's subtitle dates it 1688, and it was first published in 1693, the text given is that of 1718, which varies considerably from the version of 1693. (It may thus be taken as falling within our historical span, post-1700.) By describing the poem as 'an exercise' Prior does not mean to be deprecating, but only to acknowledge that the poem was commissioned for an occasion; for the annual tribute paid by his Cambridge college to the Earl of Exeter as descendant of one of its benefactors—a tribute which took the form of presentation to the Earl of Latin and English verses on scriptural texts. So far from thinking little of the poem Prior, by printing it first in both collections of his poems in his lifetime (1709 and 1718), seems to have had a special regard for it. It expresses a religious attitude identical with that elaborated in his *Solomon* in 1708. Particular lines in the poem can be related to passages in Denham, in Dryden's *Religio Laici*, and in Cowley. The last is the most important influence, since the metrical and stanzaic form of Prior's poem is modelled on Cowley's odes, called 'pindarick' in that they are the products of a seemingly mistaken understanding of Pindar.

11 *Wit*: in the seventeenth century and the early eighteenth meant strenuous intellection generally.

21-25 Here the inadequacy of the Pindarick rhetoric is manifest: the preposterousness of defining God by saying He is undefinable, or claiming to comprehend Him by calling Him incomprehensible, calls for an impatient slangy terseness such as the Horatian mode will accommodate but the Pindarick will not. The following strophe on the other hand (ll. 26-37) displays a baroque magnificence peculiar to the Pindarick ode as Cowley and Dryden and here Prior understood and practised it.

38-39 are the source of Watts's famous hymn:

> Jesus shall reign where'er the Sun
> Does his successive Journies run . . .

38-51, the 5th strophe, should be compared with Addison's famous hymn of 1712, 'The spacious firmament on high' (see post. p. 150). Addison's last stanza says things that Prior does not touch upon; but otherwise these forgotten lines are surely much better than Addison's cold stateliness on the same topic.

56 *NED* gives, under 'fictious': '*obsolete*= fictitious', citing this passage.

58 *new HYPOTHESIS*: may refer to Isaac Newton's *Principia*, published 1687.

60 *mighty Thoughtful, mighty Wise*: this colloquially sarcastic use of 'mighty' as adverb introduces a colloquial passage which runs to the end of the strophe. Attractive in itself, it is hardly appropriate to the lofty tone proper to the Pindarick.

65 *JARGON*: when the word came into English from Old French in mediaeval times it referred to the twitter of birds. But by the seventeenth century it meant, as it does today, gibberish or canting terminology.

74 *levelling at GOD his wandring Guess*: sustains very finely the metaphor of military siege. The guess 'wanders' like the barrel of a gun unskilfully aimed.

80, 84 Septenaries (i.e. each has 7 iambic feet—rare in English).

87 It is the prosaic word 'astonish'd' which gives wonderful power to this memorable line.

91 *Patient Victor*, because 'patient' is used in awareness of the Latin root which relates it to 'passive' and means 'suffering', is a paradox, like the oxymoron 'Eternal dy'd' in the line before, and 'bless'd with Deicide' in the line following. Because the doctrine of the Incarnation is itself a paradox, Christian writers have been able to use the rhetorical figures *paradox* and *oxymoron* to great imaginative effect. cf. Charles Wesley:

> 'Impassive, He suffers; immortal, He dies'.

101 *NED* gives, under 'perspective': 'An optical instrument for looking through or viewing objects with; a spy-glass, magnifying-glass, telescope, etc.'

The metre requires that the word be stressed on the first syllable.

112 The metre requires that 'dictated' be stressed on the first syllable.

(*And with this poem before us, must we not think that in the shift from Pindarick to Horatian, inevitable as it was—not just for Prior, Swift's poetry followed the same trajectory—and fruitful as it was for their successors, something was lost as well as something gained? I think we must.*)

p. 35 To a Lady: She refusing . . .

First published 1704, the poem appears to have been written in 1703 to Elizabeth Singer, ardent Dissenter and poetess, who took issue with Prior for his lack of seriousness as well as his High Church sentiments. Prior's wittily evasive letters to her, written in 1704, have been published.

9-10, imitated by Charles Wesley, 'Captain of Israel's Host and Guide':

> 'As far from danger as from fear
> While Love, Almighty Love, is near.'

15 *prevalence*: in the sense of 'all-prevailing'.

31 *the backward reed*: such a deliberately Latinate (Virgilian) expression, which strikes us as awkward, was in Prior's day deliberately sought after.

p. 36 A Better Answer to Cloe Jealous

Written and published in 1718, this much anthologized poem is the last in a sequence of eight in which 'Cloe' (a name perhaps given by Prior to more than one of the women he was involved with) fears that she is being supplanted by 'Lucinda', and is reassured. Prior's latest editors believe the sequence mirrors a real situation, a switch in Prior's affections from Anne

Durham to Elizabeth Cox. See the Introduction for suggestions why the poem is important. Writing in 1704 to Elizabeth Singer (see notes to the preceding poem), Prior had used the same Shakespearian allusion: 'Sweet Bardolph says Sir John Falstaffe, talk to a Body like a man of this world . . .'

The anapaestic metre permits, and almost exacts, an especially colloquial diction, as in the delightful gabble, 'More ordinary eyes'.

p. 38   An Ode
Written 1708, published 1709. Cowper's translation into Latin verse, made in 1779, was published in 1782.

ANNE FINCH, COUNTESS OF WINCHILSEA

LIFE

Anne Kingsmill, born in 1661 to an ancient family of Hampshire gentry, was lady in waiting to Mary of Modena, James II's queen, when in 1684 she married Colonel Heneage Finch, also an officer of the Stuart court, who much later unexpectedly succeeded his nephew as Earl of Winchilsea. Ever since Wordsworth's enthusiastic re-discovery of her poems, it has been usual to consider her as an isolated precursor of the Romantic Movement. But her celebration of rural seclusion has more to do with social and political, than with literary, history. Along with her scholarly and antiquarian husband, the Countess represents the non-jurors; those gentry who, bound by their oath of allegiance as well as loyal sentiment to the dispossessed Stuarts, perforce retired from public life at the Revolution. It should be noted that 'non-juror' is not the same as 'Jacobite', if the latter is taken, as it normally is, to mean 'potential rebel'. The Countess of Winchilsea died in 1720. Her *Miscellany Poems, on Several Occasions* (1713) was supplemented from MSS., in *The Poems of Anne Countess of Winchilsea*, ed. Myra Reynolds (Chicago, 1903).

p. 39   Life's Progress
8-9 By the end of the eighteenth century these lines had been transformed in oral transmission to read:

> Parnassus to the Poet's eyes,
> Nor Beauty, with her sweet surprise . . .

As the century wore on, it seems that unaffected appeals to the Hebrew Scriptures caused embarrassment. But what is more important is to recognize that at the beginning of the century such allusions seemed proper and natural to many outside the circles of the Dissenters. Thus, if the Countess of Winchilsea met the nonconformist Elizabeth Singer (as she did, and may through her have met Prior), it was at the country house of Longleat in Wiltshire, which harboured also the saintly non-juror and hymn-writer, Bishop Thomas Ken (1637–1711). Clearly there were certain circles of English society in which the supposedly extreme Whig Dissenters and the supposedly High Tory non-jurors could meet, and find themselves akin in their common allegiance to devout sobriety in private life, in a way that complicates, if indeed it does not confound, the political historian's confident herding of them into opposed camps. The Whig historians' implications that all non-jurors were concealed Jacobites, and all or most Jacobites concealed Roman Catholics, is a hoary deception that still has to be repudiated.

p. 41 *A Nocturnal Reverie*

The text is from Myra Reynolds (ed.) *The Poems of Anne Countess of Winchilsea* (Chicago, 1903); but I have re-punctuated extensively, to bring out the complicated grammatical structure.

19-20 See Jane Williams, *The Literary Women of England* (1861): 'The "Salisbury", whose strong and steady luster is advantageously contrasted with the pale and flickering sparkle of the glow-worm, was probably Lady Anne Tufton, second daughter of Thomas, sixth Earl of Thanet, who married in 1709 James Cecil, fifth Earl of Salisbury.' If this is so, then this famous poem can be dated between 1709 and 1713, when it was first printed.

32 *Till torn up Forage in his Teeth we hear* . . .: This, which is surely the most vividly authenticating image in the poem, should be borne in mind when considering Wordsworth's momentous comment (in his *Essay, Supplementary to the Preface*, 1815): ' Now it is remarkable that, excepting the Nocturnal Reverie of Lady Winchilsea, and a passage or two in the Windsor Forest of Pope, the poetry intervening between the publication of the Paradise Lost and the Seasons does not contain a single new image of external nature . . .' Leaving aside the far-reaching questions of what Wordsworth meant, and what we may mean, by 'external' and by 'nature', we need to recognize that this line appeals to a memory of what has struck, or might strike, the *ear*; and accordingly that neither in Wordsworth's usage nor in ours can 'image' be taken to mean 'mental picture', an appeal exclusively to the sense of sight.

ISAAC WATTS

LIFE

Isaac Watts, eldest child of a nonconformist schoolmaster in Southampton, was born there in 1674. He refused the offer of university education directed towards Anglican orders, and instead in 1690 entered a nonconformist academy at Stoke Newington. From that soberly sumptuous milieu (see Harry Escott, *Isaac Watts Hymnographer*, pp. 19-20) Watts returned in 1694 to the more spartan scene of Southampton, and in the next two years composed there the bulk of his *Hymns and Spiritual Songs*. (See *post* pp. 145-148.) Returning to Stoke Newington Watts, as tutor in the household of an eminent puritan, Sir John Hartopp, embarked on studies so intense that they are thought to have damaged his constitution. In 1702 he was appointed pastor of a celebrated and wealthy Independent congregation in London. From 1712 to his death in 1748 Watts was an inmate of the household of Sir Thomas Abney, and later of Abney's widow. He wrote theological and devotional works, and a treatise on logic, as well as *Horae Lyricae* (1706, 1709), *Hymns and Spiritual Songs* (published 1707, 1709), *Divine Songs ... for the Use of Children* (1715), and *The Psalms of David Imitated ...* (1719). I am sorry not to have found room for any of Watts's poems for children ('Let dogs delight to bark and bite') nor for his imitations of the psalms ('O God, our help in ages past', 'Jesus shall reign where'er the sun').

p. 43   The Hardy Soldier

The poem appears in the first edition of *Horae Lyricae* (1706) as well as in the drastically revised 2nd edition (1709), which was copied by later editions. Our text is from the 10th edition (1758).

John Cutts, Baron Cutts of Gowran (1661-1707), nicknamed 'the Salamander' for his coolness under fire, was a friend of William III and one of his most successful commanders. Namur, which had been taken by Louis XIV in 1692, was recaptured by William in August 1695. See Prior's 'An English Ballad in Answer to Mr Despreaux's Pindarique Ode on the Taking of Namure' (1695).

4 Note the allusion to Richard Lovelace's famous 'To Lucasta, Going to the Wars':

> Tell me not, sweet, I am unkind,
>   That from the nunnery
> Of thy chaste breast and quiet mind
>   To war and arms I fly.

For such a neat inversion of a Cavalier lyrist to anti-Cavalier sentiments Watts had the precedent of Milton's *Comus*.

10, 12 The imperfect rhyme (*Fears . . . Stars*) may have been more nearly perfect by the pronunciation of Watts's time. But in Watts's hymns also, as in Cowper's, imperfect rhyme is a feature too constant not to have been deliberate; and twentieth-century practice in off-rhymes, slant rhyme and assonance should make us regard it with something other than A. E. Housman's patronizing indulgence. (See his *Name and Nature of Poetry*, as quoted in the Introduction.)

19 *THRASO*: the name of a bragging soldier in Terence's *Eunuchus*. Hence the rare adjective, 'thrasonical' (vainglorious).

24 The alliteration, to convey harsh contempt, is not excessive.

p. 44 *Few Happy Matches*

The poem is dated in the 10th edition: 'Aug. 1701'.

The odds against love inside wedlock are reckoned up so remorselessly that it is not surprising Watts never married. There is no pretence that marriage vows are other than constricting: 'bands', 'chains', 'bondage', 'bonds' and 'fetters' are the words found for them.

The grotesque fancifulness of the images in lines 16-17 and 22-24, combined with the colloquial realism of those in lines 28-30 and 34-36, shows the cultivated Puritan of 1700 to be thoroughly at home in the seventeenth-century tradition of 'conceited' or 'metaphysical' wit-writing which he inherited through Marvell or Cowley from Donne.

40-42 *Sampson's young Foxes*: See Judges xv.4-5: 'And Samson went and caught three hundred foxes, and took firebrands, and turned tail to tail, and put a Firebrand in the midst between two tails. And when he had set the brands on fire, he let them go into the standing corn of the Philistines, and burnt up both the shocks, and also the standing corn, with the vineyards and olives.'

pp. 47-56 from *Hymns and Spiritual Songs*

The texts (except for 'Hosanna to Christ', p. 55) are from Selma L. Bishop,

Isaac Watts. Hymns and Spiritual Songs 1707–1748. A Study in Early Eighteenth Century Language Changes (London, 1962).

See John Julian, *A Dictionary of Hymnology* (1892), p. 1236: 'the bulk of the *Hymns and Spiritual Songs* . . . were written, and sung from MSS., in the Southampton chapel'. It is sometimes argued that poets of the present like Bob Dylan or Leonard Cohen, who compose lyrics which they say or sing to music before a live audience, have recovered an intimate relation with their public such as was lost through centuries dominated by the printed word; but in 1694–1696, at the height of the 'age of print', Watts enjoyed a relation far more intimate with his Southampton audience.

p. 47   Submission to Afflictive Providences
Job i.21 reads: 'And said, Naked came I out of my mother's womb, and naked shall I return thither: the Lord gave, and the Lord hath taken away; blessed be the name of the Lord.'

p. 48   Life the Day of Grace and Hope
The verses from *Ecclesiastes* are:

'For to him that is joined to all the living there is hope: for a living dog is better than a dead lion.

For the living know that they shall die: but the dead know not anything, neither have they any more a reward: for the memory of them is forgotten.

Also their love, and their hatred, and their envy, is now perished; neither have they any more a portion for ever in any thing that is done under the sun . . .

. . . Whatsoever thy hand findeth to do, do it with thy might; for there is no work, nor device, nor knowledge, nor wisdom, in the grave, whither thou goest.'

p. 49   The Passion and Exaltation of Christ
3-4 *smite the Man/My fellow* . . .: The compressed audacity of this paradox (Jesus as Son of Man though Son of God) was not achieved without labour. In the first edition the 4th line read, 'That's Fellow to a God'—much less surprising and powerful.

p. 50   Look on him whom they pierced, and mourn
21-22 cf. Charles Wesley: 'Strike with the hammer of Thy word
　　　　　　　　　　　　And break these hearts of stone.'

p. 51   Crucifixion to the World by the Cross of Christ
Galatians vi.14 reads: 'But God forbid that I should glory, save in the cross of our Lord Jesus Christ, by whom the world is crucified unto me, and I unto the world.'

13-16 This, the 4th quatrain, is the one omitted in *Hymns Ancient and Modern*. The emblematic elaboration of the motif of the Redeemer's blood ('His dying Crimson like a Robe') is more characteristic of Roman Catholic than of Protestant art. Watts, as an extreme protestant, might be expected to be particularly out of sympathy with the art of the counter-Reformation, as found in English poetry particularly in Crashaw. But this is not the case: Watts admired and paraphrased the Latin poems of the Polish Jesuit, Matthew Casimire Sarbiewski (1595–1640), whose odes were published in English translation by G. Hills in 1646. Known as 'the Christian Horace', Sarbiewski was admired also by Henry Vaughan (1622–95), who translated six of his odes in *Olor Iscanus* (1651). See Escott, *Isaac Watts: Hymnographer*.

p. 52   A Prospect of Heaven makes Death easy
There is a tradition (see Julian, op. cit. p. 1236) that this famous hymn was inspired by the view across Southampton Water to the Isle of Wight.

p. 53   The Church the Garden of Christ
The verses from *Song of Solomon* are as follows:
　'A garden inclosed is my sister, my spouse; a spring shut up, a fountain sealed . . .
　Spikenard and saffron; calamus and cinnamon, with all trees of frankincense; myrrh and aloes, with all the chief spices;
　A fountain of gardens, a well of living waters, and streams from Lebanon . . .
　I am come into my garden, my sister, my spouse: I have gathered my myrrh with my spice: I have eaten my honeycomb with my honey: I have

drunk my wine with my milk: eat, O friends; drink, yea, drink abundantly, O beloved.'

In a 1736 edition of *Horae Lyricae* Watts made an apology, reproduced in subsequent editions, for drawing on the Song of Songs: 'Solomon's Song was much more in use amongst preachers and writers of divinity when these poems were written than it is now.' The unabashed eroticism of the Hebrew original, and the 'nuptial mysticism' by which this was accommodated to Christian doctrine (especially by counter-Reformation Christians like Sarbiewski and Crashaw), apparently came to embarrass the eighteenth century.

See Bernard L. Manning's indispensable *Essays in Orthodox Dissent* on how the 'garden wall'd around' reflects the dissenters' conviction of 'a gathered church', i.e. a community culled from among society and *in tension with it*; as against the Anglican idea of an established Church, i.e. of church and society as coterminous.

p. 54 Miracles at the Birth of Christ
The eighteenth century was so much more aware of the precise Latinate meaning of 'condescend' that the expression 'condescended to be born' strikes us as more audacious than it seemed to them.

p. 55 Hosanna to Christ
The text is taken from Toplady's *Psalms and Hymns for Public and Private Worship* (London, 1776), and differs in some particulars from the version given as No. 16 of Book 1 of *Hymns and Spiritual Songs*. It is given here in Toplady's version to enforce the fact that hymns, like other forms of oral or folk poetry, are modified freely as they pass down through the generations (not in the eighteenth century only, but to the present day).

p. 55 The Shortness and Misery of Life
3 See *Genesis* xlvii.9: 'And Jacob said unto Pharaoh, The days of the years of my pilgrimage are an hundred and thirty years: few and evil have the days of the years of my life been, and have not attained unto the days of the years of the life of my fathers in the days of their pilgrimage.'

ANON

p. 57   *Admiral Benbow*
The text is from *Sea Songs and Shanties*, collected by W. B. Whall (4th ed. Glasgow, 1920).

Admiral Benbow, born at Shrewsbury in 1650, was engaging the French off Cartagena in August 1702 when his leg was carried away by a shot; and at that point Captains Kirby and Wade in their ships deserted him. Benbow fought his ship until the morning, when the French retired. He died of his wounds in Jamaica two months later. Kirby and Wade were court-martialled and executed.

p. 58   *The Duke of Ormond's Health*
The text is from *Sea Songs and Ballads* (ed. Christopher Stone, Oxford 1906); the ballad appeared first in Tom Durfey's *Wit and Mirth*, 1719. (Thomas Durfey or D'Urfey (1654–1723) was a prolific playwright, song-writer and poet.)

In 1702 Sir George Rooke and James Butler, 2nd Duke of Ormond (1665–1745) were repulsed from Cadiz ('Cales'), but in Vigo Bay thereafter captured or destroyed the Plate-fleet which Chateau-Regnault (line 21) was convoying home to Spain. The exact information (e.g. the name of the French commander) either assumed or purveyed by the ballad is remarkable.

JOSEPH ADDISON

LIFE

Joseph Addison (1672–1719) was the son of the Revd. Lancelot Addison, himself a poet and at one time Dean of Lichfield. Educated at the Charterhouse and Oxford, Joseph Addison was intended for the Church but was deflected into politics, where he took the Whig side and so forfeited the friendship of Pope. (In *The Spectator*, which he ran with the help of Richard

Steele, the papers devoted to the Tory squire Sir Roger de Coverley have a propagandist intention, and by being cast in a tone of contemptuous affection were probably more effective than the brilliantly trenchant satires of his political opponent, Swift.) Addison was in succession Under-Secretary of State, Secretary to the Lord Lieutenant of Ireland, and Chief Secretary of State for Ireland. In 1716 he married the Dowager Countess of Warwick.

p. 61 Ode

The text is from Helen Gardner (ed.) *A Book of Religious Verse* (*The Faber Book of Religious Verse*), 1972.

This famous hymn first appeared, unsigned, in *The Spectator* for Saturday, 23 August 1712, at the end of an essay on how to strengthen faith; it is in fulfilment of a promise given to Isaac Watts four days before (*Spectator*, No. 461), to publish on Saturdays no poetry that was not 'sacred'.

When first published in *The Spectator*, the poem was introduced by Psalm XIX, 1: 'The heavens declare the glory of God', and by these words: 'As such a bold and sublime manner of Thinking furnished out very noble Matter for an Ode, the Reader may see it wrought into the following one.'

17-24 This third strophe is crucial in the history of English devotional poetry, in that these lines confront for the first time the threat to traditional theological arguments posed by John Locke's demolition of such time-honoured notions as the music of the spheres, and by Locke's more far-reaching argument that 'reality', since it is colourless, soundless, scentless (all such sensuous qualities being 'secondary' and dependent on the observer), must be unimaginable, inhuman, and describable only in the abstractions of mathematics. Thus the 'reason's ear' in which the planets continue to 'rejoice' is above all the ear of a mathematician.

JOHN GAY

LIFE

John Gay, born at Barnstaple in 1685, was secretary to the Duchess of Monmouth when in 1714 he scored his first success with *The Shepherd's Week*, poems which derive their frail charm from the pastoral conventions which they burlesque. After *The What D'Ye Call It* came, in 1716, *Trivia*, *or the Art of Walking the Streets of London.* Having lost heavily in the crash of the South Sea Company in 1720, Gay became an inmate of the household of the Duke and Duchess of Queensberry. He published the first series of his *Fables* in 1727, and died in 1732. The three-cornered friendship between Swift, Pope and Gay was at the centre of the group of talented men which, formed during the Tory administration of 1712–13 as the Scriblerus Club, at various times included also Prior, John Arbuthnot, Thomas Parnell, and the professional politicians Harley, Earl of Oxford, and St. John, Viscount Bolingbroke. Gay was more relaxed and easy-going than Pope or Swift, and seems to have been indispensable to them for just that reason. In the same way, whereas their imaginations were powerful, his was mercurial and oblique. And yet, when in the 1720s all three were writing under Bolingbroke's generalship for the Tory opposition to Sir Robert Walpole, it was Gay's burlesque, *The Beggar's Opera*, which wounded Walpole and angered him.

p. 63 Sweet William's Farewell to Black-Eyed Susan

This ballad first appeared in *The What D'Ye Call It*, produced at Drury Lane in 1715, when it caused a breach between Gay and Richard Steele, who detected in the piece a Tory parody of Addison's heroic tragedy, *Cato*. It is indeed a tissue of parodies, as might be expected of something which Gay himself called 'a tragi-comi-pastoral farce'. This parodic intention survives into the ballad, which none the less was esteemed for 'tender melancholy', and was a best-seller when printed by itself on broadsheets. A rather unfeeling burlesque, it was itself burlesqued in a piece on the discomfiture of the Pretender in the first Jacobite rebellion, 1715.

p. 65 Polyphemus's Song

This song is from *Acis and Galatea*. Gay's libretto to Handel's music appears to have been written in 1716–17, but *Acis and Galatea* was not performed in public until 1731.

p. 66 Songs from The Beggar's Opera

Pope remarks, of *The Beggar's Opera*: 'It was acted in London sixty-three days, uninterrupted; and renewed the next season with equal applauses. It spread into all the great towns of England, was played in many places to the thirtieth and fortieth time, at Bath and Bristol fifty. It made its progress into Wales, Scotland and Ireland, where it was performed twenty-four days together; it was last acted in Minorca. The fame of it was not confined to the author only, the ladies carried about with them the favourite songs of it in fans and houses were furnished with it in screens . . .

Furthermore, it drove out of England for that season the Italian opera, which had carried all before it for ten years.'

p. 66 (1) *If any wench Venus's girdle wear*
This was sung to an air which is called 'Stingo, or Oyle of Barley' in the first edition of Playford's *The English Dancing Master* (1651). By Gay's time the air was called 'Cold and Raw', after a song by Tom D'Urfey.

p. 66 (2) *Were I laid on Greenland's coast*
These words were sung to Air XVI of *The Beggar's Opera*, which is given the title, 'Over the hills and far away', though in D'Urfey's *Pills* (1719), the same air is called, 'Jockey's Lamentation'.

p. 66 (3) *Youth's the season made for joys*
This was sung to Air XXII of *The Beggar's Opera*, which is named simply as 'Cotillion'.

p. 67 (4) *Thus when the Swallow, seeking prey*
This is sung to an air composed by Leveridge, which goes by the name 'All in the Downs' after another song composed by Gay to the same melody.

RICHARD GLOVER

LIFE

Richard Glover (1712–1785), born in London to a merchant-family, published in 1737 *Leonidas*, a blank-verse epic much extolled and internationally famous in its day but nowadays unread. In *Leonidas* probably, and certainly in 'Admiral Hosier's Ghost' (1739), Glover is providing ammunition against Sir Robert Walpole's pacific policies, and he was active in bringing down Walpole in 1742. By that time Walpole, after more than twenty years as the King's Minister, was assailed as fiercely by a powerful section of the Whigs (including the commercial interests that Glover spoke for) as by the Tories. After some lean years in the 1750s, when he wrote for the stage, Glover's fortunes improved once more after he gained a seat in the House of Commons in 1761.

p. 68   Admiral Hosier's Ghost
In 1726 Admiral Francis Hosier had been sent by Walpole to blockade the Spanish harbours in the West Indies. Prevented by his orders from taking offensive action, he saw his crews decimated by disease, and was believed to have died of a broken heart at the dishonour. Admiral Edward Vernon (1684–1757), on his own account hostile to Walpole, became a national hero when in 1739 he redeemed his promise to take, with only six ships, the Spanish fortress of Porto Bello in the West Indies. The war fever of 1739 made this the most celebrated naval exploit of the century.

HENRY CAREY

LIFE

The life of Henry Carey (1687–1743) illustrates the near impossibility of full-time professional authorship during the early eighteenth century, when the patronage system was breaking down yet authors were not protected by any effective law of copyright. The idea of literature as merchandise was long resisted; and Pope's attacks on the venality of 'Grub Street', in *The Dunciad* and elsewhere, were in effect asking for a principled independence such as economic necessity denied to all authors except the most fortunate, like Pope himself. Thought to have been an illegitimate offspring of the noble family of the Saviles, Carey seems to have taken that name only when he first came from Yorkshire to London, where he published his first collection of poems in 1713. Thereafter he wrote farces, operas in the Italian style, and burlesques (*Chrononhotonthologos* 1734, and *The Dragon of Wantley*, 1737). Though many of these were very popular, as were songs by Carey, pirate printers seem to have denied him any royalties from them. When he hanged himself in despair in 1743, he left his widow and children destitute.

p. 72 A Loyal Song

The text is from Frederick T. Wood (ed.) *The Poems of Henry Carey* (London, 1930). Wood suggests 'that it was composed by Carey in the heat of an anti-Spanish fervour in 1739, sung by him in 1740 . . . and then with the Jacobite rebellion of 1745, was seized on by the people as "a Loyal song"'. It was first published in full in *The Gentleman's Magazine* for October 1745; fifty years later a correspondent in the same omnivorous journal declared he had first heard the song at a tavern in Cornhill in 1740, sung by Carey to celebrate Vernon's victory at Porto Bello. Carey's authorship, first claimed by his son in 1795, has been disputed. The story that this hymn, the National Anthem, was composed in 1686 by Mme de Brinon to music by Lully, and sung to Louis XIV, was described by Julian in 1892, after a few contemptuous sentences, as 'too absurd for further notice'. Nevertheless, it is still current; see Nancy Mitford, *The Sun King* (New York, 1966).

p. 73 He comes, he comes, the hero comes

According to Frederick T. Wood (op. cit.), this is a song from *Britannia*, presumably the entertainment thus entitled which was given at Goodman's Fields Theatre in 1734 to honour the marriage of the Princess Anne to the Prince of Orange. Henry Bett however (*The Hymns of Methodism*, pp. 64–5) says the song was composed to celebrate—once again!—Vernon's victorious return from Porto Bello.

CHARLES WESLEY

LIFE

Charles Wesley, born 1707, eighteenth child and youngest son of Samuel Wesley the elder, was educated at Westminster School (where his brother Samuel was usher) and Oxford. In 1729 he became one of the first 'Oxford

Methodists' and in 1735-36 was in Georgia with his brother John. In 1738 he became a curate in Islington, but his congregation objected and from then until 1756 he was, like John, an itinerant field-preacher. Thereafter first at Bristol (1756-71), then in London (1771 to his death in 1788), he was in charge of the Methodist Societies in those cities. He differed from John in being more obdurately opposed to any movement by the Methodists out of the Church of England, but the two brothers collaborated in amity throughout.

Charles Wesley's more than 6500 hymns appeared in no less than 63 distinct collections between 1739 and 1786. Among these are *Hymns for Times of Trouble* (1745, occasioned by the Jacobite rebellion); *Hymns and Prayers for Children* (with John Wesley, 1746); *Hymns on his Marriage*, and *Hymns on occasion of his being prosecuted in Ireland as a Vagabond* (both 1749); *Hymns occasioned by the Earthquake* (1750, supplemented in later editions by a hymn on the disastrous Lisbon earthquake of 1755); *Hymns on the expected invasion* (1759); *Hymns written in the time of the Tumults* (1780, occasioned by the rabidly protestant Gordon riots of that year); and *Prayers for condemned Malefactors* (1785).

p. 74 He comes! he comes! the Judge severe
The text is from *A Collection of Hymns for the Use of the People called Methodists* (1876). To make this hymn on the Last Judgement, which first appeared in *Hymns of Intercession for all Mankind* (1758), Wesley adapted the preceding poem by Carey; and the Methodists sang the hymn to Carey's tune. This was neatly impudent of them, since Carey had written 'The Methodist Parson':

> Ye parsons of England who puzzle your pates,
> Who hunt for preferment, and hope for estates,
> Give over your preaching, your hopes are but small,
> For the Methodist parson has out-cut you all.
>
> What signifies learning and going to school,
> When the rabble's so ready to follow a fool?
> A fool did I say? No, his pardon I crave;
> He cannot be fool, but he may be a knave . . .

etc.

p. 75   Captain of Israel's Host and Guide

This hymn first appeared in *Short Hymns on Select Passages of Holy Scripture* (2 vols., 1762). It is based on *Exodus* xiii.12: 'And the Lord went before them by day in a Pillar of a Cloud, to lead them the way; and by night in a pillar of fire, to give them light: to go by day and night:'

9-10 were altered to their present form by John Wesley for the *Wesleyan Hymn Book* (1780).

The alteration, like others by other hands (see Julian, op. cit., p. 204) was of course for doctrinal reasons, not for euphony.

11-12 cf. Prior, 'Ode to a Lady, She refusing . . .' (*ante.* p. 38).

p. 75   O Thou Eternal Victim slain

It first appeared in *Hymns on the Lords Supper* (1745). The significantly emasculated version in *Hymns Ancient and Modern* gives for lines 1-2:

> 'O Thou, before the world began
> Ordained a Sacrifice for man . . .'

and for 8-9:
> 'Before the righteous Father's view;
> Thyself the Lamb for ever slain . . .'

These changes are not for the sake of doctrine, but in deference (one supposes) to a genteel taste which, because it shudders at the imagery of blood, has removed from the poem all its disconcerting immediacy and emblematic vividness.

p. 76   Wrestling Jacob

This first appeared in *Hymns and Sacred Poems*, 1742. John Wesley reported with pride Watts's judgment that 'that single poem, Wrestling Jacob, is worth all the verses which I have ever written'.

The source is *Genesis* xxxii.24-32:

'And Jacob was left alone: and there wrestled a man with him until the breaking of the day.

And when he saw that he prevailed not against him, he touched the hollow of his thigh: and the hollow of Jacob's thigh was out of joint, as he wrestled with him.

And he said, Let me go, for the day breaketh. And he said, I will not let thee go, except thou bless me.

And he said unto him, What is thy name? And he said, Jacob.

And he said, Thy name shall be called no more Jacob, but Israel: for as a prince hast thou power with God and with men, and hast prevailed.

And Jacob asked him, and said, Tell me, I pray thee, thy name. And he said, Wherefore is it that thou dost ask after my name? And he blessed him there.

And Jacob called the name of the place Peniel: for I have seen God face to face, and my life is preserved.

And as he passed over Peniel the sun rose upon him, and he halted upon his thigh.

Therefore the children of Israel eat not of the sinew which shrank, which is upon the hollow of the thigh, unto this day: because he touched the hollow of Jacob's thigh in the sinew that shrank.

cf. Prior, *Solomon*, Bk. 1, 607-10:

> And how could Jacob, in a real Fight,
> Feel or resist the wrestling Angel's Might?
> How could a Form its Strength with Matter try?
> Or how a Spirit touch a Mortal's Thigh?

For a student of English poetry the all but unavoidable comparison is with Francis Thompson's 'The Hound of Heaven'. The gulf between the two poems is doctrinal as well as poetic. Wesley's vision of the believer's relationship with God is altogether more tense and virile than Thompson's, and this is reflected in diction and rhythm.

39 Here, at the heart of the poem, as nearly always with Wesley, is paradox.
52 This line was reproduced by Wesley almost word for word five years later, in the famous 'Love divine, all loves excelling':

> Jesus, thou art all compassion;
> Pure, unbounded love thou art.

59 *strove*: cf. Shakespeare, *Henry VIII*, Act 2, Sc. 4:

> Or which of your friends
> Have I not strove to love . . .?

The usages 'strove' for 'striven', 'wrote' for 'written' or 'writ', 'broke' for 'broken', 'rose' for 'risen', etc. were correct by eighteenth-century usage, though discredited by the end of the century. cf. 'rose' in line 68.

74 *I halt:* in the sense of 'I limp'. From here to the end the poem is built entirely on the paradox that only when the human mind is lamed and broken by grappling with the divine, has it the strength and agility to cope with sin and Hell—'Lame as I am, I take the prey'.

JAMES THOMSON

LIFE

James Thomson, born to a modest family on the Scottish border, was educated at Edinburgh University but came to London in the 1720s and in a short time scored a notable success with the four books of *The Seasons*, in which with striking originality Miltonic blank-verse is used for the description of rural landscape and weather without any story being told. Thomson polished and expanded these poems until the 1740s. His political poems and verse-dramas are now largely forgotten, but his last poem, *The Castle of Indolence* (1748), written with deprecating and muted playfulness in Spenserian stanzas, is not much less original than *The Seasons*. Born in 1700, Thomson died in 1748; the one unconsummated love-affair in his life was unknown until twenty years ago.

Thomson was a patriotic Scotsman though he made his career in England, and we owe it to him to note his own remark: 'Britannia too includes our native country Scotland'—a sentiment, incidentally, impossible before the union of the two kingdoms in 1707.

p. 80   Rule Britannia!
This poem first appeared in 1749, in the 2nd edition of an Edinburgh songbook, *The Charmer*.

On 1 August 1740, there had been presented, in the grounds of Cliveden House, since 1737 the country seat of the Prince of Wales, a masque which the Prince had commissioned from Thomson and David Mallet to celebrate the birthday of his eldest child. In the masque Thomson and Mallet (and Thomas Arne, as musician) present King Alfred after defeat by the Danes in refuge on the Isle of Athelney, where a hermit comforts him with a spectral procession of monarchs who are to rule England greatly. The piece ends with the news that a British victory has restored Alfred to his throne;

and a blind bard then advances to sing 'Rule, Britannia'. There is little doubt that this is Thomson's work, not Mallet's; though it was credited to Thomson in Mallet's lifetime, Mallet never demurred.

Léon Morel (*James Thomson. Sa Vie et ses Oeuvres*, Paris, 1895) pointed out that the sentiments of the ode had been anticipated by Thomson in *Britannia* (1729), and also in his *Liberty* (Part IV, 1736). Throughout this period Thomson, as a *protégé* of the Prince of Wales, had been associated with the Whig opposition to Walpole; and 'Rule, Britannia' is still partisan.

WILLIAM COLLINS

LIFE

William Collins, born 1721 in Chichester, was educated at Winchester and Oxford. His *Persian Eclogues* (1742) were followed by his *Odes* (1747). He was a close friend of Thomson during the last years of Thomson's life, and soon after his death Collins was stricken with insanity; he passed the last nine years of his life wretchedly, in seclusion, and died in 1759.

p. 82   Ode on the Death of Thomson

The Thomson whom Collins's poem honours is very precisely the author of 'Rule, Britannia'. From 'druid' in the first line, through 'woodland pilgrim' in the 12th and 'sweet bard' in the 27th, to 'Briton's', two lines from the end, the poem works entirely within the frame of reference that Thomson himself, before going to his grave above the Thames at Richmond, had adumbrated: a sweeping perspective on the history of the British Isles, determined by the conviction that, centuries before Magna Carta and even before the arrival of the Romans, the inhabitants of these islands had achieved and secured political liberty. Long ago discredited, as perhaps the furthest and most audacious reach of what has been called 'the Whig interpretation of history', this conviction, while it was sincerely held, gave impressive resonance and gravity to poems like this one and the one before.

11 Though in his more ambitious odes 'allegorical and descriptive' Collins had tried to make his personifications into something that could be elaborately visualized (in ways to which the funeral statuary of the period gives a clue), a phrase like 'in Pity's ear' shows that here on the contrary personification is only a rhetorical device for achieving compact expression.

19-20 'whitening' and 'varied' show Collins attempting and achieving the effects of background in a landscape painting by Claude, as Thomson had done repeatedly in *The Seasons*.

37 *genial*: In its modern sense of 'affable', this word is much cheapened. In the eighteenth century it had some of the more elevated connotations carried since classical times by the cognate word 'genius'. Here it means chiefly 'That contributes to propagation' (Johnson's *Dictionary*, 1755).

PHILIP DODDRIDGE

LIFE

Philip Doddridge, friend and admirer of Watts, and like him a nonconformist, was born in London 1702, and educated at Kingston Grammar School. He declined the training offered him at Cambridge, with a view to Anglican orders, by the Duchess of Bedford, and went instead to a Nonconformist academy at Kibworth, where he became a minister of the Independents in 1723. In 1729 he was appointed to Castle Hill Meeting, Northampton, where he opened an Academy for the training of young men for the nonconformist ministry. His *Rise and Progress of Religion in the Soul* was a work of note in its time. He died of consumption at Lisbon in 1751. Most of his hymns were published only after his death, by his friend Job Orton. Julian in 1892 estimated that well over a hundred of Doddridge's hymns were still sung by Protestant congregations. Probably the most famous are 'O God of Bethel, by whose hand', and 'Hark the glad sound! the Saviour comes'.

p. 84   Meditations on the Sepulchre in the Garden
The text is from *Hymns Founded on Various Texts in the Holy Scriptures, by the late Reverend Philip Doddridge, D.D. Published from the Author's Manuscript by Job Orton* (Shrewsbury, 1755).

John xix.41 reads: 'Now in the place where he was crucified there was a garden: and in the garden a new sepulchre, wherein was never man yet laid.'

6 The double sense of 'end' is mordant, and finely managed.
This piece appears to exemplify a curious marriage between hymnody and the so-called 'graveyard school' in secular poetry, of which the masterpiece is Gray's *Elegy*.

p. 85   God's delivering Goodness acknowledged and trusted
The text is, as with the preceding poem, from Job Orton's collection of 1755. Orton supplies three footnotes for the benefit of the 'plain unlearned Christians' for whom, he says, these hymns were 'originally designed'.

2 Cor. 1.10 reads: 'Who delivered us from so great a death, and doth deliver: in whom we trust that he will yet deliver us.'

8 Orton notes: 'referring to the Defeat of the Spanish Armada, 1588'.
12 Orton notes: 'Gun-powder-Plot'.
20 Orton notes: 'Revolution by King William 1688'.
Every Dissenting hymn-writer, from Isaac Watts onward, has a poem celebrating these three occurrences. This illustrates how devotedly the Dissenters supported the Hanoverian succession, and the Whig interest which depended on it.

CHRISTOPHER SMART

LIFE

Christopher Smart (1722–1771) grew up in County Durham. The noble and powerful Barnard family financed him through Cambridge, where he became fellow of Pembroke in 1745 and was as famous for his learning and his verse-making as for dissolute rowdiness. He left Cambridge in or about 1749, to maintain himself as a free-lance writer and entertainer in London. There is much that is still obscure about his marriage in 1753, apparently to a Roman Catholic. Most of the time between 1756 and 1763 he was in homes for the insane, and the rhapsodic fervour of his *Song to David*, apparently composed in these years, led admirers in the nineteenth century to see in Smart an instance of how imaginative genius could survive in a rationalistic age only by escaping into lunacy. The discovery in the present century of a fragmentary long poem *Jubilate Agno* (*Rejoice in the Lamb*), undoubtedly written when Smart was deranged, gave a new lease of life to this Romantic reading of his significance. What disproves it is the splendid quality of poem after poem written while Smart was certainly sane, such as those printed here. A pension was secured for Smart, and in the 1760s he was conducting himself responsibly, but his genius was recognized by few of his contemporaries and he was financially insecure to the end.

p. 87 A Morning Piece, Or an hymn for the hay-makers
p. 89 A Noon-Piece, Or the Mowers at Dinner

For appreciation of these two poems, and a commentary on them see the Introduction. They first appeared in 'The Student, or Oxford and Cambridge Monthly Miscellany', 1750. The text is from the Muses' Library *Poems of Christopher Smart*, edited by N. Callan.

p. 91 Ode to Admiral Sir George Pocock

This first appeared in *Poems by Mr Smart* (?1763).

Admiral Sir George Pocock (1706–1792) was promoted rear-admiral of the white in 1755, and admiral of the blue in 1761. He captured Havana in 1762, and resigned from the naval service in 1766, perhaps in rancour at having been passed over for First Lord of the Admiralty. The prize-money won at Havana in any case gave him a handsome competence for the rest of his life.

2 the *White*: One would like to see a pun on Pocock's rank, but the reference seems to be to an archery target.
37-42 If Pocock on his return (he arrived at Spithead, 13 January 1763) was not greeted as a conquering hero, this is not surprising. His voyage home was disastrous, and he lost many, both ships and men.

54 'th' *increasing* poor' should be taken along with line 70, on which Smart's own note reads: 'Alluding to the Admiral's noble benefaction to the Sons of the Clergy.'

62 *Where Isis plays her pleasant stream*: that is to say, Oxford.

p. 94   Hymn XIII. St. Philip and St. James
The *Hymns and Spiritual Songs for the Feasts and Festivals of the Church of England*, to which this poem belongs, constitute an ambitious and elaborately systematic endeavour on Smart's part to adorn with hymns the entire church year as observed by the Anglican calendar. It may thus be regarded as a High Church counterpart to the Evangelical Low Church revival associated with the Wesleys. The Sunday set aside for commemorating the two apostles Philip and James is regarded by Smart (see lines 55–56) as the anniversary of the day on which these two apostles responded to Jesus's uncompromising invitation, 'Follow me'.

What distinguishes Smart as a religious poet is his consistent emphasis on God the Creator, rather than God the Judge, or God the Redeemer. Accordingly it is not easy to attend to the sense of lines 45–48, for these lines, which say that Man alone among the creatures has no home pre-designed for him, are carried on the same driving and exultant metre as has celebrated the Creator for predesigning a home for every other creature.

2 *But*: in the sense, 'except for'.

14 *genial*: Smart's 'genial spirit', even more than Collins's 'genial meads' (see the Notes to 'Ode on the Death of Thomson' p. 159), relies upon our awareness of the lofty and eloquent use of 'genial' by earlier poets, especially Milton. In the eighteenth century our impoverished sense of the word ('affable' or 'jolly') was only one part of a much richer meaning which touched on such notions as 'lustily productive' and 'peculiarly endowed'.

15-16 'painted beauties' is a highly artificial expression for 'flowers'. But this is splendidly appropriate, since Smart—like any sincerely Christian poet—sees Nature not as opposed to Art but on the contrary as itself a work of the artistically creative God.

23-24 See the Introduction for a comment on these piercing lines.

29-32 Note that 'Exercise' and 'pleasure' are here personified no less than 'Study'. See remarks in the Introduction on *prosopopoeia* as shown in the 'Strong Labour' of Smart's 'Morning-Piece'. The grouping of the three personifications in this quatrain enables Smart to say, succinctly and vividly,

something new on the perennial question of the relations between the contemplative and the active life.
43 *coney:* rabbit.
54 On the significance of this allusion to Sir Christopher Wren, see the Introduction. The line refers to St Paul's Cathedral.

DAVID GARRICK

LIFE

David Garrick (1717–1779) was the young Samuel Johnson's first pupil, and came with him from Lichfield to London in 1737. An enthusiast for Shakespeare, he effected a revolution, not just towards a more natural style of acting, but also in the social status of the theatrical professions. Himself a model of monogamous decorum in his private life, and requiring his company at Drury Lane (where he was co-proprietor and director) to observe similar proprieties, he was received in aristocratic society as well as by the intellectual elite represented by Johnson, Goldsmith, Reynolds, Boswell, Burke. He made a fortune, and was for many years hardly less famous in France than in England. His poetical works were published posthumously in 1785.

p. 98   Hearts of Oak
Composed for the pantomime *Harlequin's Invasion* in 1758, the year of the fall of Quebec, when the tide of the war with France seemed to have turned, this famous song was published in 1760 with music by William Boyce.

Boswell in his *Account of Corsica* (1768) told of singing the song to the Corsican rebels against Genoese rule: 'I sung them "Hearts of oak are our ships Hearts of oak are our Men". I translated it into Italian for them, and never did I see men so delighted with a song . . . "Cuore di querco", cried they, "bravo Inglese." It was quite a joyous riot. I fancied myself to be a recruiting sea-officer . . .' Writing to Boswell in the same year, Garrick told him 'that you should chuse my Hurly Burly Song of Hearts of Oak, to spirit up the Corsicans gave me great Pleasure! & tho I have heard it sung from North to South & East to West in England, yet I never dreamt that it would reach Corsica'.

JOHN WIGNELL

LIFE

Of John Wignell I know only that he was an actor, whose poems were published in 1762. This poem commemorates Sir Edward Hawke's defeat of the French off Belleisle, 20 November 1759.

p. 100   Neptune's Resignation
The text is from *Sea Songs and Ballads* ed. by Christopher Stone, Oxford 1906.

JOHN CUNNINGHAM

LIFE

John Cunningham (1729–1773) was born in Dublin but was of Scottish extraction. His farce, 'Love in a Mist', was published and acted in Dublin in 1747. Becoming a strolling actor, he was in Edinburgh when he published his first poem. Later publications were *The Contemplatist, a Night Piece*, 1762; *Fortune, an Apologue*, 1765; *Poems, chiefly Pastoral*, 1766. His last years were spent in Newcastle-on-Tyne, where he lies buried in the churchyard of St. John's Church.

p. 103   Morning
See the Introduction for a brief appreciation of this modest poem.

AUGUSTUS TOPLADY

LIFE

Augustus Montague Toplady, born at Farnham in 1740, and educated at Westminster School and Trinity College, Dublin, was ordained in 1762. After a curacy in the Mendips, he was vicar of Broad Hembury, Devon, from 1768-75. His last years were spent in London, where in 1776 he published his *Collection of Psalms and Hymns*. He died in Kensington in 1778. An unattractive and uncharitable character, Toplady was an extreme and rigid Calvinist (though not, it will be noted, a Dissenter). He attacked John Wesley repeatedly for the 'laxity' of his Arminianism.

p. 105 A Living and Dying Prayer for the Holiest Believer in the World

The text is from *Hymns and Sacred Poems*, ed. Sedgwick, 1860.

This famous hymn first appeared in the *Gospel Magazine* for March, 1776, where it is the climax of an extraordinary catechism which, beginning with computations to show the impossibility of paying off the National Debt, goes on to compute the impossibility of man's paying off his debt to God, supposing that he sins every second of his life:

Q: ... Now, as we never, in the present life, *rise* to the mark of legal sanctity, is it not fairly inferrible, that our *Sins* multiply with every second of our sublunary durations?

A: 'Tis too true. And in *this* view of the matter, our dreadful account stands as follows.—At *ten* years old, each of us is chargeable with 315 millions, and 36 thousand sins. At *twenty*, with 630 millions, and 720 thousand.—At *thirty*, with 946 millions, and 80 thousand.—At *forty*, with 1261 millions, 440 thousand ... (etc.).

This explains the title: the holiest believer in the world is sunk in sin unavoidably to a degree hardly distinguishable from that of the worst reprobate. The grotesque literalness with which the logic of the counting-house is applied to such non-quantifiable matters as Sin and Grace is a fearful example of how close the connections could be, for unimaginative minds in the eighteenth century, between commercialism and extreme protestant doctrine. (The hymn certainly soars free of this context of doctrinal logic-chopping; yet there is irony and pathos in its having given comfort to so many whom the ferocious and bizarre doctrines of its author would have offended.)

JOHN NEWTON

LIFE

John Newton's life is a tissue of marvels and adventures. Born in London, 1725, he went to sea with his father at eleven years old, became a convinced infidel (allegedly through reading Shaftesbury), was flogged as a navy deserter, and survived fifteen months in Africa as the dependant of a slave-trader. Converted about 1748, he spent the next six years as commander of a slaveship. In 1764, after several years ashore learning from Wesley and others, he was ordained to the curacy of Olney. From 1780 to his death in 1807 he was rector of St. Mary Woolnoth in London, a central figure in the Evangelical Movement and active in propaganda for the abolition of the slave trade. Apart from 'Glorious things of thee are spoken', hymns by Newton that are still constantly sung include 'How sweet the name of Jesus sounds', and 'Come, my soul, thy suit prepare'.

p. 106   Zion, or the City of God

The text has been reconstructed from the *Historical Companion to Hymns Ancient and Modern*. (In the current *Hymns Ancient and Modern*, the hymn is shorn of its 4th stanza, and there are other variants.) The poem first appeared in *Olney Hymns*, 1779, which contained 348 hymns of which Cowper had written 66 and Newton the rest. Newton in a preface said the collection was intended 'to perpetuate the remembrance of an intimate and endeared friendship.'

For other hymns by Newton, and an appreciation of Newton as poet, see the Introduction.

WILLIAM COWPER

LIFE

William Cowper, born 1731 at Berkhamsted, was educated at Westminster school and called to the Bar in 1754. After some happy years and friendships, the strain of an examination for public office unhinged a mind which had always been hypochondriac, and in 1763 in a first fit of madness he attempted suicide. His earliest hymns date from the period of his recovery, when he withdrew (1765) to reside at Huntingdon. In 1768 he removed with his companion Mary Unwin to Olney in Buckinghamshire, where it is not clear whether the pastoral ministrations and devoted friendship of Newton were a help or a hindrance to his condition. His insanity recurred from time to time. His first volume of poems (1782) was followed by *The Task* (1783). He removed to Weston in 1786, and to East Dereham, where he died in 1800. The death of Mrs. Unwin in 1796 plunged his last years into 'fixed despair' of which the strange and appalling poem, 'The Castaway', is the expression. Most rigorously logical and honest of Calvinists, Cowper explained the curse of his melancholia by supposing that God had singled him out for a unique fate, in that, having once elected to 'save' him, God subsequently cancelled the election and consigned him to perdition.

p. 108   *This ev'ning, Delia, you and I*

The text is from Cowper, *Poetical Works*, ed. H. S. Milford, 1905; 4th ed. (enlarged), 1934; with corrections and additions, 1971.

The poem, written as early as 1752, was first published by James Croft in 1825, long after Cowper's death, along with other poems to Delia. Delia was the poet's first cousin, Theadora Cowper. Their marriage was forbidden by Theadora's father because of their near kinship. 'But', says Croft, 'though frustrated in their wishes, they did not cease to love, nor occasionally to meet.'

The poem is very clearly related to Prior's 'Ode' (p. 38), which Cowper later translated into Latin. Cowper loved and admired Prior; see passages in his *Letters*, and also 'dear Mat Prior's easy jingle', in 'An Epistle to Robert Lloyd, Esq.' (1754). In *The Book Collector* for Winter 1973 Mr. Charles Ryskamp published a slightly different version, lately discovered by him with other Cowper poems in an 18th century commonplace-book.

p. 109   *Light Shining out of Darkness*

The text is from Cowper, *Poetical Works* (ed. cit.), but re-punctuated. The poem first appeared in Newton's *Twenty-six Letters on Religious Subjects . . . by Omicron* (1774), and was not definitely assigned to Cowper until publication of *Olney Hymns* (1779).

If Toplady's 'Rock of Ages' is habitually taken in a more comforting sense than its author intended, the same is even truer of Cowper's 'God moves in a mysterious way'. For there seems no doubt that the poem is related to Cowper's attempt in 1773 to drown himself in the Ouse at Olney, either as a reflection upon it in 1774 when Cowper was recovering his sanity or else, more poignantly and probably, as a presentiment of it in 1772. According to Newton, it seemed to Cowper's disturbed imagination 'that it was the will of God he should, after the example of Abraham, perform an expensive act of obedience, and offer, not a son, but himself'. (Of course both Cowper's hymn and Toplady's *are* comforting; but the comfort they give is much more austere than is commonly recognized.)

21 See *John* xiii.7: 'Jesus answered and said unto him, What I do thou knowest not now; but thou shalt know hereafter.'

p. 110 *Welcome Cross*

The text is from Cowper, *Poetical Works* (ed. cit.), but re-punctuated. This hymn first appeared in 1774, in a hymn book for use in the chapel at Bath of the famous Evangelical Countess of Huntingdon. There it precedes, as in *Olney Hymns* it follows, 'God moves in a mysterious way'; and we can presume it was composed about the same time, out of the same horrifying set of circumstances.

20 *a cast-away*: The weird light cast forward on to Cowper's last and most terrible poem, thus entitled, will be obvious.
21 See *Hebrews* xii.8: 'But if ye be without chastisement, whereof all are partakers, then are ye bastards, and not sons.'

p. 111 *Self-Acquaintance*

The text is from Cowper, *Poetical Works* (ed. cit.). It first appeared in Newton's *Twenty-six Letters on Religious Subjects . . . by Omicron* (1774).

p. 112 *The Shrubbery, Written in a Time of Affliction*

The text is from Cowper, *Poetical Works* (ed. cit.). Written 1773, the poem first appeared in 1782.

21 *prospects*: Cowper's learned propriety is apparent in the way this word is taken first as a forward-looking vista through space, as in a landscaped garden, then as a forward vista through time.

p. 113 On the Trial of Admiral Keppel
The text is from Cowper, *Poetical Works* (ed. cit.). Written 1779, the poem was not published until 1890.

The court-martial of Keppel began on 7th January 1779, and ended with his acquittal on 11th February.

p. 113 The Modern Patriot
The text is from Cowper, *Poetical Works* (ed. cit.). The poem was first published in 1782.

Cowper told Unwin on 27th February 1780 that he had destroyed verses with this title aimed at Edmund Burke, having read a speech by Burke which seemed to promise a change of heart. Cowper's editors speculate that the poem was reconstructed by Cowper and given a new application, to the Gordon Riots of June 1780.

It looks as if Cowper could not forgive Burke his sympathy with the cause of the rebellious American colonists. But Burke was in any case at this time launching his campaign against Warren Hastings, Cowper's friend and schoolfellow, for alleged peculation on a grand scale in India.

p. 114 Joy and Peace in Believing
The text is from Cowper, *Poetical Works* (ed. cit.), but re-punctuated. It appeared in *Olney Hymns*, 1779.

15 See *Matthew* vi.34: 'Take therefore no thought for the morrow: for the morrow shall take thought for the things of itself. Sufficient unto the day is the evil thereof.'
25ff. See *Habakkuk* iii.17, 18: 'The Lord thy God in the midst of thee is mighty: he will save, he will rejoice over thee with joy: he will rest in his love, he will joy over thee with singing.

I will gather them that are sorrowful for the solemn assembly, who are of thee, to whom the reproach of it was a burden.'

p. 116 Jehovah our Righteousness
The text is from Cowper, *Poetical Works* (ed. cit.). It appeared in *Olney Hymns*.

See *Jeremiah* xxiii.6: 'In his days Judah shall be saved, and Israel shall dwell safely: and this is his name whereby he shall be called, THE LORD OUR RIGHTEOUSNESS.'

The doctrine is uncompromisingly Calvinist, and impressively so.

p. 117   Exhortation to Prayer
The text is from Cowper, *Poetical Works* (ed. cit.), re-punctuated. The poem is from *Olney Hymns*.

13-16 See *Exodus* xvii.11: 'And it came to pass, when Moses held up his hand, that Israel prevailed: and when he let down his hand, Amalek prevailed.'

Julian says, reasonably: 'really not a hymn, but a fine instruction on prayer'.

p. 118   Prayer for Patience
The text is from Cowper, *Poetical Works* (ed. cit.), but re-punctuated. It first appeared in *Olney Hymns*.

p. 119   Welcome to the Table
The text is from Cowper, *Poetical Works* (ed. cit.), but re-punctuated. It first appeared in *Olney Hymns*.

p. 120   Love Constraining to Obedience
The text is from Cowper, *Poetical Works* (ed. cit.), but re-punctuated. It first appeared in *Olney Hymns*.

The subtle but crucial and persisting truth in the Calvinist position has never been stated more firmly than in this poem, particularly its penultimate stanza: the Christian does good not because it is his duty to do so, but because (by God's grace) he wants to.

23 See *Romans* iii.31: 'Do we then make void the law through faith? God forbid: yea, we establish the law.'

p. 121   The Valley of the Shadow of Death
The text is from Cowper, *Poetical Works* (ed. cit.). It first appeared in *Olney Hymns*.

p. 122   The Negro's Complaint
The text is from Cowper, *Poetical Works* (ed. cit.). Written March 1788, the poem was taken up by the abolitionists and widely publicized. It appeared in *Stuart's Star*, 2 April 1789, and in *The Public Advertiser* of the same date; in *The Diary*, 6 July 1790; in *The Arminian Magazine*, September, 1790; and in other widely circulated magazines.

p. 124   Sweet Meat has Sour Sauce
The text is from Cowper, *Poetical Works* (ed. cit.).

Written March 1788, it was not published until 1836. Cowper said he wrote the verses to the tune, 'Malbrouck s'en va-t-en guerre' (i.e. 'For he's a jolly good fellow').

p. 125   A Good Song
The text is from Cowper, *Poetical Works* (ed. cit.). Written c. 1792–93, it was published in *The Anti-Gallican Songster*, 1793.

This is printed from an anonymous broadsheet by Cowper's latest editors in an Appendix; they describe it as 'one of the loyalist counterblasts to Paine's *Rights of Man*, pt. II', which was published in 1792; and say that 'Cowper's authorship is probable . . . since he expressed much the same sentiments in his letters'. If the poem is Cowper's, it shows clearly how a very learned and secluded poet could, when he wanted to address a wide public, avail himself of a popular form.

p. 126   To Mary
Written in the autumn of 1793, and published posthumously in 1803, with the omission of lines 37–40 (no great loss, and indeed no loss at all) which were not printed until 1900. The text is from Cowper, *Poetical Works* (ed. cit.).

These verses to Cowper's companion Mary Unwin, already far advanced in senility, are one of the most striking examples in the language of how a stanza-form apparently foredoomed to sentimental monotony can be redeemed by a poet who cleaves relentlessly close to the painfulness of the relationship he seeks to commemorate.

9-16 These lines, which by their fidelity to homely fact decisively raise the poem above the level of a sentimental exercise, were not achieved without labour. A surviving manuscript preserves the infinitely weaker version:

> Thy needles, once a shining store,
> Discernible by thee no more
> Rust in disuse, their service o'er,
>   My Mary!

> But thy ingenious work remains,
> Nor small the profit it obtains,
> Since thou esteemst my pleasure gains
>   My Mary!

Note that, pious poet as he was, Cowper does not pretend that the conditions of total dependence on the one hand, of senile decay on the other, are anything but desolate.

EOGHAN RUADH O SUILLEBHAIN

LIFE

Eoghan Ruadh O Suillebhain (Owen Roe O'Sullivan), born in south-west Munster in 1748, wandered the roads of southern Ireland as an itinerant schoolmaster. In or about 1780 he either enlisted or was 'pressed' into the Royal Navy, and sailed from Cork for the West Indies in a vessel which joined the fleet of Admiral Rodney. On the morning of 12 April 1782 Rodney sighted the French under De Grasse; the French line was broken as they passed southwards near Dominica; and at sunset De Grasse struck his flag. O'Sullivan's ode, written within hours of the engagement, was promptly presented to Rodney, presumably in hopes of thereby buying the poet's release from service. This did not happen, for O'Sullivan is later found in the army back in England. Released, and back in Kerry, he died wretchedly in 1784. This is the only known English poem by one who has been called 'the sweetest singer of Gaelic verse in his time'. O'Sullivan's poems in Irish show that his true allegiance was Jacobite, as might be expected. In certain Gaelic-speaking families of the Irish gentry the sons through several generations served with the armies of France, Austria or Spain against Hanoverian and protestant Great Britain; and during the War of the American Revolution (1776-83), American naval forces were commanded by the Irishman John Barry.

p. 130 Rodney's Glory
The text is from Daniel Corkery, *The Hidden Ireland* (4th impression, Dublin 1956).

PRINCE HOARE

LIFE

Prince Hoare (1775-1834), born at Bath, began life as a painter, and exhibited in the Royal Academy 1781 and 1785. From 1788 to 1797 he wrote prolifically for the London stage, mostly musical farces. For the last 35 years of his life he pursued yet another career, scholarly and academic, as secretary to the Royal Academy.

p. 133 The Arethusa
The text is from *Sea Songs and Ballads*, ed. Christopher Stone (Oxford, 1906). It is said to have been sung first in W. Shield's opera, *Lock and Key*, 1796.

The *Arethusa* (32 guns, commanded by Captain Marshall in Keppel's fleet) encountered *La Belle Poule* off Ushant in June 1778. The poem is quite misleading, for the French ship had the better of the engagement. The writing of course is wretchedly bad.

HENRY PHIPPS, EARL OF MULGRAVE

LIFE

Henry Phipps, first Earl of Mulgrave and Viscount Normanby (1755–1831) had a respectable career as a soldier, and subsequently as a statesman. He was to become secretary for foreign affairs in the last ministry of Pitt (1805–06).

p. 135 '*Our line was form'd*'
The text is from *Sea Songs and Ballads*.

This song commemorates Admiral Lord Howe's victory of 1 June 1794, when he took the Channel Fleet to engage the French 500 miles off Ushant. The grotesquerie of 'timber toe' seems brutal, but it is the mutilated sailor who speaks.

WILLIAM BLAKE

LIFE

William Blake, born 1757 in London to a tradesman of extreme dissenting persuasion, was apprenticed engraver in 1771. After the *Poetical Sketches* he devised a way of marrying his two arts, and his subsequent volumes are not printed in the ordinary way but 'engraved'. His startling originality in this and other ways meant that he was known and esteemed in his lifetime by only a very small public indeed. In his religious convictions, his political sympathies and his philosophical assumptions, as these are made apparent with daring boldness of invention but something less than perfect clarity at first in lyric and later in epic forms, Blake was consciously at odds with virtually all the attitudes that had governed eighteenth-century civilization in England, various as that was. Thus it is only proper that this anthology should end with him.

p. 137 Song

The text is from *The Shorter Poems of the Eighteenth Century*, ed. by Iolo A. Williams (London, 1923). The poem first appeared in *Poetical Sketches* (1783), a volume printed at the expense of Blake's well-wishers, the Revd. Henry Mathew and the sculptor John Flaxman.

The 'prince of love' who, for all his beneficent splendours, is revealed at the end as a cruel tormentor of the singer, is on the one hand Apollo, Greek god of the sun and also of poetry; but he is at least equally, to those who have read Watts (as Blake had), Jehovah or Yahweh, the God of the Jews who in the Song of Solomon, so Christian commentary supposed, figures as the radiant bridegroom entertaining his beloved in his gardens. Thus, in this poem which Blake is said to have written before he was fourteen, if the Graeco-Roman or neo-classical element of English Augustanism is rejected, so is the Hebraic element. For Watts, the Wesleys, Cowper, the two elements supported each other; Blake rejects both, though in fact in his career as a whole it is the authoritarian father-figure of Jehovah which is rejected with most contumely.

10 The elaborately artificial diction of this line, though it may be thought appropriate in conjunction with the named neo-classical deity Phoebus, is strikingly at odds with the diction of the rest. If we nevertheless find this adroit and effective, we shall tend to suppose that the merging of Phoebus Apollo with Jehovah is a profound insight splendidly imagined; if on the contrary the line strikes us as bizarre and at best heavy-handed, we shall tend to find in the poem as a whole not a dazzling ambiguity but a glorious muddle.

There is little doubt what Blake's first sponsors thought. Mathew, in his Advertisement to *Poetical Sketches*, warned the reader: 'Conscious of the irregularities and defects to be found in almost every page, his friends have still believed that they possessed a poetical originality which merited some respite from oblivion.'

INDEX OF AUTHORS

Addison, Joseph, 61
Blake, William, 137
Carey, Henry, 72, 73
Collins, William, 82
Countess of Winchilsea, *see* Finch, Anne
Cowper, William, 108–126
Cunningham, John, 103
Doddridge, Philip, 84, 85
Earl of Mulgrave, The, 135
Finch, Anne, 39, 41
Garrick, David, 98
Glover, Richard, 68
Gay, John, 63, 65, 66
Hoare, Prince, 133
Newton, John, 106
O Suillebhain, Eoghan Ruadh, 130
Prior, Matthew, 31, 35, 36, 38
Smart, Christopher, 87, 89, 91, 94
Thomson, James, 80
Toplady, Augustus, 105
Watts, Isaac, 43–55
Wesley, Charles, 74, 75, 76
Wignell, John, 100

INDEX OF TITLES AND FIRST LINES

Admiral Benbow 57
Admiral Hosier's Ghost 68
All in the Downs the fleet was moor'd 63
Arethusa, The 133
As near Porto-Bello lying 68
A trader I am to the African shore 124

Better Answer to Cloe Jealous, A 36
Brisk Chanticleer his matins has begun 87

Captain of Israel's host, and guide 75
Church the Garden of Christ, The 53
Come all ye jolly Sailors bold 133
Come cheer up my lads, 'tis to glory we steer 98
Come, O thou Traveller unknown 76
Crucifixion to the World by the Cross of Christ 51

Dear Cloe, how blubbered is that pretty face! 36
Dear Lord, accept a sinful heart 111
Duke of Ormond's Health, The 58

Exhortation to Prayer 117

Few Happy Matches 44
Forc'd from home, and all its pleasures 122

Give ear, ye British hearts of gold 130
Glorious things of thee are spoken 106
God moves in a mysterious way 109
God save great George our King 72
God's delivering Goodness acknowledged and trusted 85
Good Song, A 125

Hardy Soldier, The 43
Hearts of Oak 98

178

He comes, he comes, the hero comes	73
He comes! he comes! the Judge severe	74
Here's a health to honest JOHN BULL	125
Hosanna to Christ	55
Hosanna to the Royal Son	55
How gaily is at first begun	39
How sweet I roam'd from field to field	137
Hymn XIII. St. Philip and St. James	94
If any wench Venus's girdle wear	66
Infinite Grief! amazing Woe!	50
In such a Night, when every louder Wind	41
In the barn the tenant cock	103
In yonder grave a druid lies	82
I rage, I melt, I burn	65
Jehovah our Righteousness	116
Joy and Peace in Believing	114
Keppel, returning from afar	113
Life is the Time to serve the Lord	48
Life's Progress	39
Life the Day of Grace and Hope	48
Light Shining out of Darkness	109
Living and Dying Prayer for the Holiest Believer in the World, A	105
Look on him whom they pierced, and mourn	50
Lord, who hast suffer'd all for me	118
Love Constraining to Obedience	120
Loyal Song, A	72
Man! Foolish Man!	31
Meditations on the Sepulchre in the Garden	84
Miracles at the Birth of Christ	54
Modern Patriot, The	113
Morning	103
Morning Piece, Or an hymn for the hay-makers, A	87
My God, how perfect are thy ways!	116
My soul is sad and much dismay'd	121
Naked as from the Earth we came	47
Negro's Complaint, The	122

Neptune frown, and *Boreas* roar	58
Neptune's Resignation	100
Nocturnal Reverie, A	41
Noon-Piece, Or the Mowers at Dinner, A	89
No strength of Nature can suffice	120
Now the winds are all composure	94
Ode, An (The merchant, to secure his treasure)	38
Ode on the Death of Thomson	82
Ode (The spacious firmament on high)	61
Ode to Admiral Sir George Pocock	91
Oh, happy shades—to me unblest!	112
On Exodus iii.14	31
On the Trial of Admiral Keppel	113
O Thou Eternal Victim slain	75
Our Days, alas! our Mortal Days	55
Our line was form'd, the French lay to	135
O, we sail'd to Virginia, and thence to Fayal	57
O why is Man so thoughtless grown?	43
Passion and Exaltation of Christ, The	49
Polyphemus' Song	65
Praise to the Lord, whose mighty Hand	85
Prayer for Patience	118
Prospect of Heaven makes Death easy, A	52
Rebellion is my theme all day	113
Rock of Ages, cleft for me	105
Rodney's Glory	130
Rule Britannia!	80
Say, mighty Love, and teach my Song	44
Self-Acquaintance	111
Shortness and Misery of Life, The	55
Shrubbery, The	112
Sometimes a light surprizes	114
Songs from 'The Beggar's Opera'	66
Song (How sweet I roam'd . . .)	137
Spare, gen'rous victor, spare the slave	35
Submission to Afflictive Providences	47
Sweet Meat has Sour Sauce	124
Sweet William's Farewell to Black-Eyed Susan	63

The King of Glory sends his Son	54
The merchant, to secure his treasure	38
The Sepulchres, how thick they stand	84
The spacious firmament on high	61
The Sun is now too radiant to behold	89
The twentieth year is well-nigh past	127
The wat'ry god, great Neptune, lay	100
There is a Land of pure Delight	52
This ev'ning, Delia, you and I	108
This is the feast of heav'nly wine	119
Thus saith the Ruler of the Skies	49
'Tis my happiness below	110
To a Lady: She refusing . . .	35
To Mary	127
Valley of the Shadow of Death, The	121
We are a Garden wall'd around	53
Welcome Cross	110
Welcome to the Table	119
What various hindrances we meet	117
When Britain first, at Heaven's command	80
When Christ, the seaman, was aboard	91
When I survey the wond'rous Cross	51
Wrestling Jacob	76
Zion, or the City of God	106